The Little Man

A Father's Legacy of Smallness

By ANDY LITTLETON

NEW HERALD PUBLISHING LLC - TUCSON, AZ

Printed in the United States of America

First Printing, 2019

Cover Art by Olena Stefuk
Back Cover Photo by Aaron Menken
Cover Design by Stephen Yeakley
Photos Courtesy of Andy, Leroy, and Betty Littleton unless
otherwise noted

New Herald Publishing

newheraldpublishing@gmail.com

Contents

*Dedicated to my mom,
my dad's sweetheart Betty Littleton,
for all that she contributed
to my dad being the man that he was
and to me becoming the man I'll be.
Thank you!*

"It's alright to be little bitty.
Little ole' town or a big ole' city.
Might as well share.
Might as well smile.
Life goes on for a little bitty while"

Alan Jackson - Little Bitty

Intro
A Train to Oregon

His name was Leroy. He strode the Tucson streets in silence. Grey bearded. Flannel clad. Thin and tall with a full head of hair combed, but falling over his forehead. Headed nowhere in particular. No doubt a mysterious man to many. One of those regular sightings to others. He was the type that makes you smile and feel that all is all-right in the world.

"There's ole' Leroy, walking his rounds again."

I saw him a few times a week myself. He lived a stone's throw down the street in a brown and yellow house with a fragrant rosemary hedge around the driveway. A stunning green Model A Ford with yellow wheels sat parked in the shade of the carport. All the neighbors knew the house. Few knew it was Leroy's.

Seeing Leroy walking about meant much more to me than to anyone else. You see, he was the most important man in my life. Leroy was my dad. Sometimes I was the one walking with him on a crisp cool Arizona winter evening. I was the one in a t-shirt and jeans. I look like a younger version of him.

We loved our quiet walks together. Now it's just me. On the crisp winter evenings I wear one of his favorite Pendleton flannels.

My Quest

My first-ever sabbatical break from work began about a month after my dad died. The break had been on my mind for some time, but I had no idea how providential the timing would be. Few get the luxury of taking sabbatical. It's usually a time of rest and renewal. My sabbatical became a quest. A quest to understand the mark left on my soul by Leroy Littleton, the quiet walking man. My dad.

My dad had been on my mind more than ever, even before we found out he'd had cancer for years and only weeks to live. A year before the terrible news I wrote a chapter's worth of musings about my dad. The ways he differed from the other men I looked up to in life up to that point struck me. I didn't know what to do with my writings at that time. He was a private man. He'd have been uncomfortable with the attention of even a simple blog post. As I mourned I wondered how to process it all. I re-read my chapter and knew I wanted to write more.

I had an opportunity. I had eight weeks away from the regular rhythms of life. I modified my plans so I could immerse myself in thoughts about my dad. In our world, the loudest voices get the most attention and the greatest following. My dad was quiet, but worth listening to. He's not the only one. My mind swirled in grief, but one thing was clear. My dad was a gift. I'd share him with others. My dad was not alone. There are others like him whom we all should value more. There are people he connected with whom we should engage with and love.

To remember him well, there were specific places I wanted to go and experiences I hoped to have. I wished that my dad and I had spent more time in Oregon in my adult years. I was born in Oregon. We lived in a small logging town called Lebanon until I was five or so. I only retained a few scant memories of our old home town, but heard about it throughout my life. My dad chose Lebanon as home after having moved there as a kid. He liked Bisbee, but it didn't feel like home to him. He'd only lived there when he was very young, outside of coming back for a short run of high school. He loved Oregon.

His family moved where the railroad had work to do, and Oregon was where the work was plentiful. His family retained their homestead on the outskirts of Bisbee. They would return there in time, but my dad had become an Oregonian. The Southern Arizona landscape was a bit too dry and barren for his taste. He'd come to love the forests and streams of the Pacific Northwest as a grade-schooler. He liked to gaze from the top of a grassy hill and see shades of green stretched out for miles before him.

Lebanon served another important role in Leroy's life. It's the town where he became a man. It's where he forged his own way when he returned from deployment in Germany during the Vietnam War. The area is breathtaking; ideal for walking and driving about. These were his favorite pastimes. The forested hills provided a sheltered space for him to explore and clear his mind. The howl of freight trains cutting through the forests comforted him. They reminded him of the best times of his childhood.

Leroy's father was a welder with the railroad. Leroy played between the tracks and train cars. He explored the small towns where the railroad placed the family's boxcar. Trains and the tracks were the fascination of Leroy the inquisitive boy. He never would be much of a talker, but when he'd light up and get chatty...these were the topics that got him started. Near the end of his life, he lay in hospice care in Tucson, Arizona. The white board in his room read: "Things I like to talk about: Trains, Oregon, my granddaughter Abby, and Bisbee, AZ."

I wanted him to show me these places once I grew old enough to care. We only lived a couple hours from Bisbee most of my life, so we visited there together from time to time. He showed me around the family property. We looked for arrowheads in the fine dirt under the gnarled desert brush together, as he'd done as a boy. We visited beautiful Arizona landmarks he'd heard of. It's never enough when you love someone, but we did experience much of Arizona together. Unfortunately we ran out of time to explore Oregon as father and son. Foolish me...I thought we had another twenty years or so.

I planned my sabbatical to stir up memories and connect with the experiences my dad loved to talk about. I mapped out three trips with times to reflect and write during each one. The first and last would be a couple hours from home in Bisbee and the surrounding areas. The second would be the most important. I'd finally go back to Oregon. That's where insights about my dad would stand out. I would see his favorite part of the country for myself. I would look out for people that reminded me of him on my journey.

I knew that I had to take a train up the west coast. My dad's love for trains made that the obvious choice. Amtrak's Pacific Coast Starlight was one of the trips my family had hoped to take together. It would guide me down the very tracks my dad had explored, and through one of the towns he lived in. My dad was an avid walker. I began to plan some long walks upon which I'd ponder my journey the way he pondered his. I considered the long walk to Portland from Lebanon to visit a couple of friends of mine in the city. My mom convinced me that my dad loved long walks, but wouldn't have walked that route in a million years. He didn't like the city. He wouldn't walk down the highway by choice. She redirected me down a stretch of the Oregon Coast, and between the towns of Sodaville and Lebanon. These were walks my dad actually took in his younger years.

As I contemplated my Oregon plans on my first day trip down to Bisbee, I felt there was only one element missing. My dad had bought his first new truck in Oregon in 1968.

He talked about it often. It was his very own, fresh-off-the-assembly-line, 1969 Ford F-250 Ranger. He always described it as "a real good truck." He'd say, "We outta get one of those to pull the Model A around with."

The Model A was the car his uncle gave him as a fifteen-year-old in Bisbee. When he left for Oregon he left it behind broken down in the yard. Luckily the family kept rusty the old car. It lay out amidst hundreds of automotive carcasses strewn throughout the desert brush. He and I towed it out of there with the help of my uncle when I was in my mid-twenties. We got it home and stripped it down. We peeled off four layers of dusty upholstery. We removed and organized every accessory part. Our friend Fred Swanson hauled it to Denver and finished the restoration for us. The Model A and the F-250 were the two favorite cars he'd owned. Now we had one of them all fixed up and under the carport.

The F-250 though, was the vehicle that belonged to my dad's Oregon experience. He kept all the paperwork for it. I still have a clipping of him on the front page of the Lebanon Express in it. A sports car rear ended-him and wedged it's front end up under the truck bed...his moment in the spotlight. He loved that truck. If you asked him which vehicle he wished he'd kept he'd always talk about the F-250. He sold it for the sole reason of achieving a crazy goal he and my mom had. That goal ended up landing us back in Arizona for the rest of our lives.

The day my dad made the front page

I milled through a box of memories dad left for me. As I shuffled through all the F-250 documents, I had the idea of trying to find one up in Oregon to drive around. At first I thought of trying to borrow one. Who in the world would let a guy from Arizona come out and borrow their classic truck? I had another idea. I hopped onto Lebanon's craigslist page in a moment of pure stupidity. To my surprise I found one that was only one year off, made the year he bought his. It was so close to his too...the exact same body style, it had the "Ranger package" like his did. It also had surprisingly low miles, looked to be in decent shape, and only cost $1200 cash. The color did it for me. Green. My dad's truck was green and white, but what were the chances of finding a green one for sale? The fact that is was for sale when and where I needed it seemed incredible to me.

I called the number and got ahold of the seller, an old farmer named Dwight. To my surprise, Dwight wanted to help me out. He liked what I was doing he said. He held on to the truck for over a month without deposit. He even brainstormed how to make it roadworthy with me over the phone on several occasions. As if that weren't enough, he decided he'd take a few days off of his farm work to help me get it ready to roll. He even offered to come pick me up at the train station. My trip had come together. It was almost too good to be true. On May 11, 2018 I caught an early morning flight out of Tucson. I had to catch the morning Amtrak in Los Angeles, bound for Albany, Oregon.

Dwight

This trip was about remembering my dad. But to be honest, meeting Dwight had become one of my most frequent meditations. He had made the process of long distance auto purchasing seem like a walk in the park. I told him I was taking a journey of writing about and remembering my dad. I told him my dad had bought his brand new '69 F-250 when he lived in Oregon and loved it. It was the truck my dad always bemoaned that he should have kept. My story must have connected with Dwight. He wanted to help.

Dwight's truck was very close to the one I rode around in as a kid. It was even closer to where my train ride ended. I wanted to get it more than anything. I rationalized. I considered that I could either rent a car and stay in hotels or I could buy a vehicle that I could sleep in. Dwight's F-250 came with a faded brown and yellow aluminum camper shell. All I had to do was park and crawl in the back. I couldn't beat the price or the odometer reading. It had been a farm truck for much of it's life. Dwight bought it off a neighbor he knew for years who he called "Herman the German." It hardly saw the highway he claimed.

I continued to mill the decision over and over. On top of it's utility on my trip, I could use it for work back home. If sold my small furniture shop's old broken-down Toyota "space van" I could have the money in hand. The real reason, of course though, was sentimental. I had the chance to experience the towns my dad loved from the cab of the truck he experienced them from. I wanted to have that experience. I wanted to do more than remember my dad. I wanted to understand his perspective.

The key to this plan was Dwight. Could I trust the guy? Was he even up for the fact that I wasn't coming to his state for over a month? The next phone call I had with him included him informing me of several minor issues with the truck to consider. The radio didn't work. One of the headlights was burned out. All that he followed with a great tip. A good guy he knew named Dennis, over in the town of Stayton, had a wrecking yard full of old Fords. Dwight thought old Dennis would have everything we'd need. This I doubted.

When I called Dennis though, he said...

"Oh yeah...I got all kinds of stuff for those trucks. I can get you a headlight for $5, good tires on some Ford rims for $250, and I think I have a newer battery around...$30 for that."

I told him I got his name from a guy named Dwight.

"Oh yeah, I know Dwight", he said about as casually as one says "no more coffee, thanks" to a waitress.

So far, Dwight seemed to have a pretty good average.

When I told Dwight I was in Arizona, and wasn't coming to Oregon for a month, he hardly blinked an eye.

"I'll just hold on to it for ya, I'm in no hurry."

I ventured... "What kind of deposit do you need?"

Alarmed by the question he interjected..."Deposit! You ain't even seen the truck, you don't wanna be sendin' me no money for it yet! Why don't you just come up here when you can and take a look?"

Of course that was fine with me. I hadn't sold my van to get the money at that point. It sold days later for cash, but if Dwight had asked me to wire him some money I don't know where I would have dug it up.

At any rate, ole' Dwight didn't seem like the type of guy that was trying to take someone for a ride. I told him I would come to take a look at...and planned to buy his truck if it all checked out. I would arrive in Albany on the train on May 13th...Mother's Day.

"Sounds like a plan." he said.

My trip had all come together. The train, the town, the truck. Now for the hard part. It was time to dive fully into remembering my dad. It was time to see things from his perspective.

On Sunday the 13th, late morning, the Amtrak train rolled into the Albany Depot. It squealed to a stop and a few of us weary travelers trudged toward the exits. I eased into a shaded bench, inhaling in my first breath of Oregon air since my childhood. It was a warm and sunny spring day. The kind of day my dad loved. Not too hot. Not too cold.

I was beyond curious about the man on his way to pick

me up. Every vehicle that entered the parking lot had my full attention. Many vehicles passed me by, but none seemed right. A small sedan...no. A minivan...highly unlikely. At this point only two of us were still at the station. A nearly new and sparkling blue Ford truck eased the corner. It's driver wore an old straw hat. I knew it was Dwight from a distance. He headed right for me.

As he drove up Dwight flashed a crooked-toothed smile and invited me to throw my bags onto the rear seats.

"Hey, it's good to meet you Dwight! Andy Littleton."

This was the first time I had mentioned my last name throughout our correspondence. We shook hands.

"So, how ya doin'?"

"Oh, I've been down in San Antonio picking up an airplane." He replied, sounding a bit tired-out.

"You know how to fly right?"...he inquired with ease.

My eyes furled a bit. Mind you, my eyes felt as if someone had stuffed them with lead weights. I had hardly slept on the train. Holding my eyes open feels awfully akin to holding open the hood of a Ford truck...yet they react to this question.

"No..." I sheepishly ventured.

"You're here for the 250 right?"

"Yea..."

"The Cherokee 250...the airplane?"

"No...the F-250...the Ford...the old truck." I stammered.

The side of his mouth cracked slowly open. A slight grin revealing two neighboring crooked and inwardly depressed teeth. I cocked my head and tried to wrap my mind around what he was saying. I wondered if I'd contacted a disorganized old man. He forgot what I called about perhaps. It'd been well over a month since we'd first spoken over the phone. He had two "250's." The Ford sold a long time ago. He thought I was buying an airplane I couldn't fly and didn't want to. A slight feeling of panic began to well up within me. He looked happy.

"Heh heh" he chuckled quietly. "You really went for that one."

Now he was beaming...very proud of himself as he gazed at the road ahead. I learned that Dwight had a sense of humor. Dry and subtle. You could miss his jokes if you weren't paying attention. That reminded me of my dad.

The remainder of this book will weave in and out of my my writing trips to Lebanon and Bisbee. The chapters are arranged around the order in which these characteristics became evident in Leroy's life.

I

Little, Stupid, Slow

Leroy grew up feeling very small. He was the eldest son of Alberta Scott Littleton, whose parents died when he was young. At a young age Alberta went off to war and seems to have attempted to erase his old identity thereafter. We have no idea why. When he arrived in the Bisbee area, it was under the name Leroy. No one in the area knew the details of his past that we know of, not even my grandmother Dorthea. We've found no records, and he had no interest in talking about it. Leroy Sr. and Dorthea had five children. Leroy Jr. was in the middle between Freida and Mable and Judy and Jake.

My grandfather poured his pain upon his namesake. He often belittled and berated his eldest son. Leroy Jr. became the object of many a cutting insult. He may have expected the most from him. He may have seen his own shortcomings in him. Whatever the case, the words "stupid," "ugly," "slow," and "nobody" haunted my father. They hit hard from his father's lips. He crept into his head through a perpetual inner voice. One day I, as a belligerent teenager unaware of his painful story, would hurl the same words at him to my shame. His siblings didn't endure the same assault.

Leroy and his siblings; Mabel, Judy, Frieda and Jake

If there was one phrase that my dad used to describe himself, that I've never forgotten, it was "the little man." He used it almost always in the negative. There were, you know...the big guys, those with power, money, and know-how. They were the bosses and those with "brains." Then there was "the little man" the "half-wits," the "broke", the ugly...like us.

"The little man just can't get a break," he'd say from time to time.

I always rebelled against his appraisal of himself. On the one hand, I simply didn't want it to be true of him, and by extension I suppose, true of me. On the other hand, I knew he sold himself far too short. I had evidence too.

People loved him in every circle he inhabited. From time to time, he would take me to work with him at Grant Road Lumber when I was a kid. Everybody there, his co-workers, the bosses, the guys in the hardware store, the "yard dogs," the millwrights, and the customers, enjoyed him and wanted to be around him.

Growing up, I always wished that he saw in himself what everyone else saw in him. I pushed so hard against his self-appraisal. When he urged me to go to college so I wouldn't be "like him," I determinedly entered the workforce to prove that being "like him" was actually admirable.

As I've grown and become a man myself, I've battled with my feelings about my dad. Without question, my self-doubt and low self-esteem are an inheritance. I wish he would have taken more responsibility for his situation in life, and that he'd stood up to more people and in-so-doing showed me how. But I remain grateful for the legacy he left me. A legacy that I've discovered, so few men receive.

I've read a lot of books on being a man in my lifetime. In my line of work I've been a part of many events promoting "healthy masculinity" and have helped plan a few. What I've noticed is that most of the events platform some sort of macho man; a man who exhibits great confidence and conviction, strength and resolve. My dad exhibited none of those things. He was on nobody's list to be featured at the next men's conference. Yet, he's left an indelible mark upon the world that I'm not sure he ever realized he was leaving.

Interestingly, in my circles I've also seen many "great men" fall, but not my dad. I watched him rise (the writing of this fills my eyes with tears). I watched my dad press further and further into his convictions as the years went by. I watched him draw steadily closer to my mom through the trials that they faced. I watched him grow increasingly content though the life he dreamed of always managed to elude him. I watched his impact on others grow as he moved from being a middle-aged man to an elder in his workplace and community. I watched deep faith develop within him in spite of his incessant doubts.

The more I've reflected on my dad I've realized that we all need to learn from him. I need to learn more from him than I did while I had him living just down the street. I have concluded that being a "little man" may be the best possible aim.

So, Leroy grew up feeling very small. In fact, he did have

his challenges. He wasn't able to eat for the first ten days of his life because of a blockage between his esophagus and stomach. He underwent surgery after ten days that resolved the issue, but it likely had lasting effects. He may have sustained brain damage due to being nutrition starved during those critical days. Research hadn't borne out the connection between nutrition and the brain back then, so people assumed he was "just slow."

It took Leroy longer to process an idea or figure something out than most people. He learned to work around the disability as much as he could. If you went out to eat with him, he'd order "whatever she got" unless he had been to the restaurant enough to remember the meal he liked. His father had little patience for him and pointed out his slowness into his adulthood. He didn't understand why his son couldn't "get a move on" like everybody else.

He also had a certain set of physical challenges. He was kind of a scrawny guy. He had a heart murmur for years of his life that worried him. In time he developed an essential tremor that kept him from doing fine detail work with his hands. He told me, that when he was first old enough to work, it took a lot of convincing to get a mill boss to hire him. He didn't come across like he could physically handle the job. Once he got hired though, he proved a reliable and hard working employee. Sadly he'd struggle to achieve promotions to the higher paying jobs he'd aspire to having throughout his life.

Leroy also never fully related to the vision of manhood that a lot of people around him assumed. His dad and younger brother talked gruff and vulgar, shot guns, drank beer, and smoked cigars. Leroy adopted none of those practices. It wasn't that he thought they were wrong per se. It was that the attitude that accompanied those activities was the same one that belittled him, and he wanted nothing to do with it. He also had an artistic side. He was musical, and taught himself to play the guitar well enough to get him invited into several bands. His mother was a painter, and he liked to watch her.

He loved to visit craft fairs and observe the ideas of others that could inspire him. He collected unique pieces of material, discarded remnants of wood and metal, with the hopes that someday he'd have a workshop where he could turn them into something nice to share.

Needless to say, when he received his draft letter during the Vietnam War, Leroy was not one of the battle-ready. He wished there was a better way to solve the problem. He wished for a way that didn't involve sending him and other young men in there with guns and tanks. The army stationed him in Germany and trained him as a fireman and tank operator. He was willing to do his duty, but hoped with all he had not to see combat. The war ended before they called his unit to action to his deep relief.

In the military though, he'd seen past the Western United States and came away with some more perspective. He'd also made some decent money. He bought himself a nice camera, and started taking photos to scratch his creative itch. When he got back to Oregon he bought himself a brand new Ford F-250 (his first new vehicle), some nice instruments so he could play in local bands, and a property of his own off Lacomb drive near Lebanon, that he called "the swamp." He was becoming his own man.

Soon after he'd returned from Germany his dad was having a drink at the house, and invited Leroy to have one with him. He'd actually tried out a bit of that life with his buddies in the military. He had decided that it wasn't only "not him," but that it could lead you to do things you might really regret. No doubt, he'd felt a bit of his father's bad side rise up in him in those moments, and it scared him. He'd also had time to reflect on the type of man he was and wanted to be. Leroy had always kind of acquiesced to his father, but this time he didn't. He looked at his father and said,

"If that's what it means to be a man, drinkin' and killin', then I don't want to be one."

With that he left, and pursued what it might mean to

be a man outside of his father's shadow, yet beset with his own set of weaknesses. What he learned led him to be a beloved member of his community as he embraced many characteristics worthy of aspiring to. He became a beloved dad to me, grandfather to Abby, and husband to Betty Lee.

2

Dedication

"I'll try...to love only you.
And I'll try...my best to be true.
Oh darlin'...I'll try"
- Alan Jackson

On the only Saturday I spent in Oregon on my trip, I decided to call an audible.

I had taken the F-250 to the one exhaust guy in Albany to install manifold gaskets. Albany is where I decided to spend my evenings since Dwight offered his couch free of charge. Albany is about twenty-five minutes northeast of Lebanon. The truck had once been re-assembled gasket-less. It sounded like an old tractor running for its life every time you accelerated down the street. Dwight and I started the work ourselves. The bolts turned, but creaked a wicked sound. The first backed out slow, but all the way to my relief. The second bolt started slow, began to turn and snapped.

"Looks like those are stainless steel...I don't know why in the world they'd use stainless steel bolts."

This baffled Dwight. He'd seemed worried about this part of the project, and had hunted the yellow pages for exhaust shops. The time had come to take it to the professional he'd tracked down. Luckily he was willing to get it done the next day. We did a lot of the work ourselves and this fight wasn't worth it. I picked up a little Jeep from the only rental car company in town to get me around for the day. Dwight needed to get back to work on the farm.

Going the professional route turned out to be a very good move. It ended up taking the poor guy three and half workdays to get the bolts either backed out or drilled out. I popped in on him a few times. Cursing and banging echoed between the old fenders. He would alternate between a welding torch and his socket wrench to try to avoid breaking the bolts. More than any of us bargained for!

My original plan included a walk down the Oregon coast on my last day of the trip. I also wanted to visit a couple friends in Portland once I had wheels. I assumed I'd package all that into one trip in the old Ford. Now, truck-less, I decided to take advantage of the "unlimited miles" on my little borrowed Jeep. I'd make the trek to the coast in the gas saver. Not only that, I decided to make a whole day of the trip and not try to couple the coast with anything else. Portland could wait.

I stopped by the exhaust shop one more time before they closed for the weekend. He wasn't even close to done. I made my way back to Dwight's to crash on his couch again. I slept well for the first time on the whole trip. My body had acclimated to the cushions and the hard spot between the cushions.

I awoke shortly after sunrise, well before Dwight or his son, who was in town from college in Salem for the weekend. I showered quick and snuck out before anyone could rope me into a conversation. The morning greeted me cool and dense with mist. The green trees leapt from the landscape against the backdrop of soft gradient grey. I queued up a country music station and hit the road.

My rental car got me along just fine, far better than the F-250 would have. I still wished I had my hands wrapped around the old truck's steering wheel. I let my imagination stir. I envisioned my dad in his mid-twenties. He drove his next-to-brand-new F-250 down the same winding roads. At this point he worked at one of the Lebanon lumber mills, played bass or banjo in a band, and kept himself busy I'm sure. Busy as he may have been, he wasn't tied to any relationship. He didn't even have a girlfriend. My dad, free to do as he pleased whenever he pleased. As long as he showed up for work, nobody would question him.

I imagined him taking a weekend getaway to the coast. He hopped into the truck. Windows down, he wound through the layers of mossy forests. He picked up speed. The land spread into overlapping farms, which lay like a giant doormat before the majestic, distant, tree-covered mountains. He re-entered the forest, slowing for the turns as the road narrowed. I imagined his favorite music on the radio. He had upgraded the truck to have a turn-dial Philco mounted in the dash with a single speaker. He turned up ole' Ernest Tubb and Chet Atkins...high enough to make out the notes above the rush of misty breeze that pummeled his face between the old Ford's quarter glass windows. I imagined him in the thick green-and-black flannel coat he used to have. He wore his dark rimmed glasses...gazing silent across the lush green scenery he loved so much.

It wasn't too difficult to imagine it all. The same lush landscape lay before my silence. The same misty rush toyed with ripping my hat off my head as it bellowed through the cabin of the little rental Jeep. Alan Jackson, George Strait, and Brooks & Dunn's distinct melodies danced above the subtle roar. And for the first time in as long as I could remember...I was all by myself, free to do as I pleased with my time...even if it was only for a couple weeks. My wife and daughter weren't with me on this trip. No one asked me to put the windows up, or turn the music down, or play their type of music, or to talk about what was on their minds.

Then I began to smell the ocean air. Seagulls soared overhead. Finally I could see the water peeking through windows between the trees. The mist transformed to tiny droplets of rain and hung thick over the Pacific, so thick I could hardly make out the ships anchored close to the shore.

I parked at the first little lot I found, grabbed a rain jacket, and started walking south. I didn't have a destination in mind. I didn't know how long I would be walking. I just walked. I stopped to take a picture when I saw something interesting. I filled my pockets with little treasures: seashells, agates, and driftwood to take back to my daughter. Then I walked some more. I began to miss my dad intensely and deeply. He would have loved a long walk with me on this beach. I would have loved it too.

A recurring thought wove in and out of my trip to the coast. I contemplated it throughout my five-hour silent walk on the pebble-strewn beach. My dad chose to lay aside so much to become a loving husband to my mom, and a supportive daddy to me. My mom didn't like country music, or the windows down with wind messing up her curls. I didn't want to visit Oregon as a kid. I wanted to go do cool stuff in California. The two of us filled up, not only his weekends, but also his weeknights...and morning quiet times. No more was he free to do as he pleased.

Then I realized that a lot of men I've met would refuse to lose such amounts of freedom. Many men demand that their families bend to fit their own desires. Others will choose their freedom even if it costs them their family. Many refuse ever to be "tied down" in the first place. Others promise to share their lives, but break their promises in the pursuit of reconstructing their lost freedom.

I wondered if my dad thought any of that through. How did he decide to move from having his own freedom unrestrained to dedicating his life to the lives of others he chose to love?

When describing my dad as a dedicated man, I do not mean that he never "cheated" on my mom. He didn't. But his dedication wasn't mere restraint. It consisted of much more. What I mean is that he chose to trade in his freedom for a life dedicated to living with and for his wife and kid. If a comfy car ride without music were what my mom wanted, he would joyfully choose to do that. If I wanted to check out some stores with cool clothes instead of enjoying a quiet walk on the beach, he'd be right there with me. He tried to understand while he was at it.

He still loved his long walks and invited me along, but he got to take them far less often. He still loved his old country music, but it became his companion only on his short solo rides to work and on weekend errands he ran by himself. I can't recall him enjoying a lazy weekend alone again in his life. But he went to the grave living with the express goal of making sure my mom received the care she needed, and making sure we both knew that he loved us.

I don't mean to say that he had to suffer the loss of his freedom. He truly preferred to be with those he loved, especially my mom and I. But even in such gain there is a real loss. To give your life to others, even others you'd prefer to be with, places great demand upon yourself. Demand to give. Demand to sacrifice.

I don't know if my imaginations of my dad taking the long drive to the coast correspond to any actual events. But I do know that he once had freedom. He had declared his own path out from under his father, and for a time his life seemed only to belong to himself. To dedicate his life to Betty Lee Bowles, whom he met at the Odyssey Book Shop in downtown Lebanon, was a choice that came with a real cost. That cost he never regretted, but it was a cost nonetheless. To be the father of an often self-centered son, who demanded so much and gave back so little, came at a great cost as well. A cost he counted and found worthwhile. A cost many run from.

Days before my trip to the coast, before arriving in Albany, I had been trying to sleep through the night in a train car seat. I had an assigned seat in coach on the Amtrak. It reclined back a few inches, but not enough. I couldn't seem to figure out the angles. Train rides are sweet if you aren't in a hurry. The seats are far more spacious than those on airplanes. Not having been on a passenger train since childhood, I had forgotten how much you could walk around and acquaint yourself with the whole train. Your seat is spacious, but you don't have to live in it.

After hours of trying every possible bodily configuration in my seat, I decided to check things out on foot. Dawn was breaking and I had heard that we could see Mount Shasta from the train by morning's light. The viewing car was a few cars ahead of mine, so I decided to go experience that for the first time. I hadn't ventured there for the view of the California coast. The cars are all lined with windows, but the viewing car's windows are huge and the seats face outward.

To my surprise, I found that some of the people in coach had bypassed my seat comfort dilemma. As I walked through the other passenger cars, I realized that some passengers sleep on the floor. When I arrived at the viewing car, folks were laying all over the place. One guy had adopted a four-top dining table. He made it like a bed with sheet and blanket. There he was, sprawled across the surface like he owned the place.

To my surprise there were still some front row seats on the east side of the viewing car. That was exactly where I wanted to be in case we came upon Mt. Shasta soon. Another man wandered into the car and sat down close by. A lady from Oregon came to the area too. She had a lot to say about herself. She struck up a conversation with a young guy who'd either started drinking at five in the morning or had been drinking all night long. He had a lot to say too.

As the sunlight peeked over the horizon we could see a snowcapped mountain standing prominent in the distance. The man who'd sat down near me asked if we were getting out first glimpse of Mount Shasta. He had heard the same thing I had about the morning view. I told him I wasn't sure, but I thought I'd have my camera ready just in case. That was his plan too, but his cell phone battery had weakened and was about to die. Our phones were the only cameras we had. We ended up tag-teaming the photography and I texted him photos once he lost battery power.

Once we'd passed Mount Shasta the conversation continued. His name was Jeff, and he and his wife Lisa were traveling together. He wasn't too sure where his wife had gone off to at the moment. He also wasn't looking. The landscape had his full attention. A woman came hunting through the viewing car. She was looking for him.

"Why didn't you answer your phone?" she asked. "We just passed Mount Shasta!"

Jeff explained himself...the dead phone...how he got caught up talking to this guy from Arizona who's heading back to his hometown to get an old Ford truck and remember his dad. She let him off the hook, but suggested they head to the dining car for breakfast. Soon after, I followed suit.

When I walked into the dining car, Lisa spotted me and waved me over.

"Want someone to sit with?"

I had learned the night before that you will sit with someone in the dining car, whether you want to or not, so I gladly accepted the offer. Jeff and Lisa were from California. Now retired, they were taking the opportunity to explore together. This train ride up the coast hit the right stride for them. Lisa had to get caught up on my story, and what my plans were up in Oregon. I told them all about it, and they adopted me for the rest of the train ride.

Back in the viewing car, Jeff and Lisa helped me spot one of the tiny towns where my dad lived when he was a kid. My grandfather's job for the Southern Pacific Railroad took them from station to station in the mountains of Oregon. The family lived on the rails in a modified boxcar part of the time. Oakridge was one of the towns they lived in. I'd seen that we would travel through the center of town on my itinerary. They would have parked my dad's boxcar home right next to the tracks we would travel across.

"Andy! Oakridge! Over here...this side!" I heard Lisa calling.

I hurried over just in time to see the little train station. The whole town blew by in a moment.

My favorite thing about spending time with Jeff and Lisa on the train became watching them interact. You could tell they had their differences but that they had grown to love each other deeply over the years. It wouldn't surprise me if they'd had some very trying times. Most of us do in some measure, but they had made it this far. Now retired, they were content to travel around together and build their shared experiences. The same became true of my parents' later years.

The truth is that my mom and dad had some pretty rocky years themselves. Their early days in Oregon were full of hard work on top of having and getting used to raising a son. For the most part though, life was pretty good. They had no idea the challenges that lie ahead. They had no idea that they would end up taking a risk that would result in them almost losing everything.

The lumber industry in Oregon declined in the mid-eighties. The Lebanon plywood mill closed and my dad and many others lost their jobs. To survive my parents moved from my dad's property on Lacomb drive and downsized. My dad took a job fifty miles away that paid far less. My mom taught night classes at two different community colleges. It was all taking a toll. They decided to try a crazy idea they had.

They sold their new property on "windy hill" and bought a used Jamboree motorhome. They planned to travel the country, which neither of them had been able to see much of, and look for a new home. Money was tight, but my dad would work in each state to try things out. When we found a good job in a place we liked, we would settle down.

We started by heading up to Washington where dad worked harvesting cranberries in the autumn. Cranberries are grown in "bogs" that are flooded and churned to release the berries from the vine. He wore waist high rubber boots and helped corral the floating berries and load them into trucks. Then we moved down the Long Beach Peninsula and he worked in the oyster beds. Workers wire baby oysters into oyster shells that other workers plant in the bay at high tide. My dad would help deliver the bales by raft into the bay where they would rock the raft to unload the bales. My mom hated this job because my dad couldn't swim. Every day she anxiously awaited his return.

Before leaving Oregon my dad saw an advertisement for a technical school in Tucson, Arizona. He had heard that computer programming was the future. His parents were also celebrating their fiftieth wedding anniversary that year in Bisbee. He and my mom decided to head down the West Coast to Arizona to see my grandparents and sign up for the school. My great aunt lived in Tucson, so we could park the motorhome for free while he got a certification. The plan was to keep moving after that.

Unfortunately, that plan failed. Soon after we got to Tucson, the school went bankrupt. All my dad had to show for his time there was a toolbox of electrical testers and an empty bank account. My mom had found a job at a high school library to help while he went to school. My dad picked up some day labor gigs to help us recover while he looked for a better job. As if that weren't enough, my mom started to experience abdominal pain. A surgery and medical bills officially halted our progress. We sold the motorhome.

We ended up living in a run down mobile home park called The Shady Haven. Our neighbors would get drunk and into fights with each other on a regular basis. In time my dad got a job at Grant Road Lumber making a fraction of what he had made back in Oregon. The stress that came with these events threatened to drive a wedge between my parents. Stress, disappointment and embarrassment set it. I remember my parents arguing over money. I remember the word divorce yelled in the heat of a bitter argument.

These events could have signaled the end for my parents. They could have walked away from each other and the troubles that they were experiencing as a couple. Instead, they persevered. In some ways, they buckled down, and made better decisions. My mom continued to work full time at the high school library until retirement. Dad attended community college in the evenings, which challenged him more than I'll ever understand. After a lot of hard work he achieved his certification to be a machinist.

They didn't fix all their problems. They learned to accept the other person in their faults more often than not. Many times my dad would tell me that we had to love my mom, even though we didn't understand why she did what she did.

"She's a pretty good mama, and she loves us." He would remind me.

His simple words would calm me down, and his gentle reminders always rang true. I knew she loved us.

Later in their life my parents decided that they wanted to make sure they traveled together. It had always been their dream. It was why they tried out their crazy idea in the first place. They didn't get everywhere they wanted, but they sure gave it their best effort. They explored almost every road in the West, according to my mom, even some of the dirt roads. They saw most of the western National Parks together. They sought out train rides like the Cumbres and Toltec and the Durango and Silverton. They drove through as many States as possible. My dad would take pictures along the way. My mom would figure out the route and points of interest to visit. They also developed an ever-increasing bond of love. The photos of their trips were always sweet. They enjoyed being together more than anything.

On vacation at Monument Valley

That joy overflowed into their everyday lives as well. My wife and I would smile as we watched them walking slowly down the street, hand in hand. One time we met them in Downtown Tucson for a show at the theater. We said our goodbyes afterward, and amidst all the commotion, the two of them walked away from us...and gently their hands came together. Dedicated still. They made it hand in hand.

On my second writing get-a-way to Bisbee I decided to catch a movie at the Bisbee Royale. The Royale is an old church converted into an entertainment venue and theater. It sits nestled amidst the storefronts and miner's cottages in Tombstone Canyon. The Royale could be a bit of metaphor for the town itself. Years ago, when the town boomed, men flocked to get good jobs in the mines. They set up their little cottages on the canyon cliffs with hopes of making a good life

27

for themselves and their families. The churches followed in hopes of saving people's souls and encouraging people to live by the "Good Book." Today, downtown Bisbee's churches are either standing as relics with a few remaining faithful folks, or are being repurposed into large homes or venues. The town in general has the reputation for being free of oppressive moral constraints like the Bible's laws these days.

I love Bisbee. Like my dad, I have an artistic side; so all the artistic folks who've come and inhabited the old spaces in Bisbee are a welcome addition in my mind. I also love the surrounding areas, where many of the folks who used to frequent Old Bisbee still live. Decades ago the bulk of the churches moved out to the surrounding areas.

Many of the residents of Old Bisbee seem to be there in search of some kind of freedom, and I can understand that quest. It seems that many of the old residents, who live in the outskirts, are trying to hold on to something familiar that's always seemed good and right to them. I can understand that desire too. I tend to feel very in the middle.

Sometimes I wonder how far apart we all really are. At the theater I found myself surrounded by the downtown Old Bisbee crowd. The movie highlighted several social issues. It made you think about race, sexuality and relationships. The hero of the movie was a married man with a loving wife, often away from home and on the road. In one pivotal scene an attractive woman approaches the hero in a bar. We all could see what was coming next, but were hoping we were wrong. She consoles him, and places her hand upon his. His eyes connect with hers. He enfolds her hands with his, and the theater gasped. A woman in a hushed voice exclaimed "No, don't do it!"

There is something good about dedication that seems to run deep within our souls. You don't just find it in thriving churches where people get pumped up about morality and the "Good Book." It is more shared than we realize, even in the churches now converted into bars and clubs. There's a hope most folks have, that promises will be kept. There's an aversion most folks also have, to infidelity in all its forms.

My dad stands as an example that promises can be kept. And they aren't just kept by those touting their personal fidelity.

Often promises are kept best by those standing quietly... hand in hand with their families.

I know as well as anyone, that my parents' relationship fell quite short of the "ideal". There were plenty of disappointments and a laundry list of uncomfortable moments. None of us were blind to the issues of the others. I would venture to say that our family's flaws were more obvious than most. No one ever told me that they wished they had my family, or that we came across as the perfect family to them...not once. I thank God for that. We learned to love each other without the pretense of worthiness.

My mom you see, loved to eat out very much. Cooking felt like a true chore to her, and she worked as much as my dad for most of her life. In my younger days a fried chicken sandwich at McDonald's on the way home made her day. Later in life a stop at Subway for a turkey sub after a long workweek did the trick. A Saturday breakfast out made life a little more sunny later in life when money wasn't as tight.

My dad didn't hate going out to eat either. Believe me, he knew the chances of having a delicious breakfast at Sunny Side Up were much higher than the chances of us doing all that work at home. Despite that, his natural disposition lent toward saving rather than spending. He would get concerned if we ate out too much, and would offer a cautionary word from time to time. Several times this very topic catalyzed a tense discussion or argument in our home. I liked my mom's perspective, as it lent to me eating tastier food.

The last time this argument occurred, it began in the living room. My dad had been feeling a little off, but it seemed like a bug of some kind. My mom had been pondering the options... going out for a delicious breakfast down the street, or "slaving away in the kitchen" to produce something less exciting. The choice was clear. She wanted to go out to eat. She proposed the idea to my dad, who suggested they just stay home. My mom's assumption was that he had money in mind. She let him have it. Told him off you might say. She couldn't understand why he had to be like that and couldn't just "live a little". He held his ground, to her absolute frustration. They never went out to eat again. Their next trip out was to the urgent care. Then to the hospital.

My mom was guilt stricken. She hadn't been considering him in the conversation. She wasn't wondering how he might be feeling, or why he might be feeling that way at the time. On top of the lack of consideration, she'd been unkind. She'd assumed the worst about the man who'd always loved and cared for her. Now the diagnosis was cancer and the prognosis wasn't good.

In the hospital room my mom broke down in my dad's presence and apologized. How could she have been so selfish? How could she have been so blind to the pain and discomfort he'd suffered lately? She confessed it all, and poured out her heart to him. In his usual way, he quietly gazed her way and listened to everything she spilled out to him. Then he took her hand and gently spoke.

"I forgive you B. I love you."

What I've learned from my dad is that dedication comes through forgiveness. There's no other way. People really don't deserve our hearts and trust. For that matter, none of us deserve the open hearts of others if we're honest. Forgiveness though, is a powerful force. My mom speaks of this moment with my dad more than she speaks of moments when they both got things right. It is great when we love each other well, but we feel loved most, I suppose, when we acutely realize we don't deserve the love we're being given.

3
Restoration

"They don't make 'em like they used to."
- Every American male born before 1970

I finally got back in the driver's seat of the old F-250 after it had been at the exhaust shop for days. I dropped off my rental Jeep in downtown Albany and hitched a ride from one of the agency employees over to the shop. The mechanic was gone but had left the keys. A guy that shared his shop told me the truck was ready to roll. Later investigation proved him wrong. The amount of time the truck spent in the shop derailed my plan to finish working on it myself. To keep things on schedule I asked the exhaust guy to swap the spark plugs and change the oil. I drove away with a few new plugs but mostly old ones that were loose. He changed the filter but hadn't drained the oil itself. The new manifold bolts were present but not tightened down.

At the time I couldn't tell. I have no idea if he failed to finish or lied about finishing. I had to leave first thing in the morning to get back home to Arizona in time to see my daughter graduate from elementary school. It all looked put together, and it ran better than before. I was off.

I rolled down the windows and enjoyed the, now quieter,

purr of the engine. My first stop was a car wash. I blasted off the layers of dust that had accumulated over the twenty years the truck sat under a walnut tree on the farm. Then I took Dwight's back road route through Albany, which opens up into a beautiful expanse of Oregon farmland once you get out of town.

The air rushed fresh and cool through the cabin. The sun began to settle over pine-covered hills. All I had left to do before my trip home was to prepare the old truck for camping. I didn't have much to load into the old brown and yellow aluminum camper shell. I brought only a few pieces of luggage on my trip. Then I had thrifted a few essentials to keep me comfortable and warm on the way home.

I wanted to get the truck all set up that night. Dwight had made a standing offer that I could either crash on his couch while I stuck around, or that I could camp out back on his farm. At first the couch was the only reasonable option in my mind. Then Dwight drove me to the edge of his property. The back end of his farm, the view shrouded by a mass of trees and berry bushes, bordered on the Santiam River. He had created an amazing grass landing on the river's edge, complete with a boat ramp, fire pit, and a porta-potty. It was a perfect place to camp. I decided to get used to camping by staying back by the river as soon as I got the truck back. I only had one night left to do so.

The Santiam River from Dwight's boat ramp

I began by spraying the bed of the truck out with a hose one more time. I tried to get every wasp's nest and spider's web out of the corners and crevices. Then I laid out my supplies on Dwight's creaky old redwood porch. I had a tool kit to assemble. I found a grey and purple 80's lunch box, and one of every tool I knew I needed for the truck, while shopping at the local thrift stores.

Dwight emerged from his mobile home wondering why I had his whole porch covered with junk. Upon further inspection he approved. I had picked up just about everything I would need if something needed fixing along the way. I organized my kit and stashed it down in the F-250's built-in tool box. The tool box is one of my favorite features. It even came with the two original keys!

Next I made sure that I had all my camping supplies; a yoga mat I had picked up to buffer between my body and the hard metal-ridged truck bed, a pink sleeping bag I reasoned I could give to my daughter when I got home, some LED lamps, a camouflage pillow to go with the sleeping bag, and a vintage red and white cooler for snacks. I had to fit all of that into the bed with my spare parts, an extra set of rims and a spare tire clad rim, a gas can, water jugs and the luggage I had brought with me on the train.

Dwight returned to the porch from watching the news and announced that he wanted to treat me to dinner out. I had everything together, for the most part, but had planned on having another couple hours of prep. I was starving though. Dwight was generous with his food at home but usually ate microwaved Jimmy Dean breakfast sandwiches for dinner. One time it was the sausage sandwich. Another time it was the angus. Every time it was greasy. I had mentally prepared myself for another one of those. Going out sounded like a great alternative. I also assumed I would never see the guy again so I took him up on his offer. He declared that this place in town had the best hot-roast-beef around. I had no idea how serious he was about this.

He drove me over in one of his other Ford trucks. He had a few, two of which he still drove. We pulled into a crowded parking lot. The restaurant had the "been around awhile" feel that I love...lots of wood grain, well-worn seat cushions, menus with fraying edges. The place wore western theme from top to bottom.

When we sat down he beckoned the waitress over with raised hand.

"We'll have two hot-roast-beef plates Sweetheart." He announced with finality.

Apparently I didn't have a choice. This hot-roast-beef was a "must have" in his mind. He also found the waitresses to be "hot" and a "must have". He clearly wasn't encountering her for the first time either. She entertained his subtle advances. He liked more than just the hot-roast-beef at this place.

I liked the hot-roast-beef. It was exactly as it should be - white bread, deli-grade sliced roast-beef in the middle, mashed potatoes and gravy plopped on top for good measure and a side of canned green beans. Standard...but familiar in a good way. Exactly what you should order at a small-town dive. Exactly what you should eat with a guy like Dwight.

As we awaited our plates, Dwight re-hashed the details I needed to know about the old truck. The distributor cap needed to remain at a certain degree off top-dead-center. This he had told me about twenty-five times throughout the last few days. Apparently he should have said it a few more times because I promptly forgot the details.

I tried to get to know a little more about him before leaving. He was chock-full of tales of adventure. He had maneuvered out of many sticky situations. He had chased many women. He commented that he liked one of the other waitresses more than ours. He asked if I thought she was good looking. She was in her fifties. I gave him a nod. He made sure she was at the cash register when we checked out.

We got back to the farm late. Dwight told me he was thinking about taking me out to a bar for some old country music, but they looked closed when we drove by. He really wanted to celebrate I guess. I was getting dreary-eyed. The end result for me...I was too tired to set up camp by the Santiam in the dark. I decided to crash on the couch for one more night. That way I could shower in the morning and hopefully get some better sleep. Then I would make up my losses by grabbing a Hungarian breakfast in town at Novak's. That's where I wanted to eat. The waitresses didn't flirt and the food was amazing. They served you a warm miniature cinnamon roll to hold you over between making your order and receiving your meal.

I woke up bright and early in the morning before Dwight, which was saying something. I loaded up my toiletries and duffle bag, fired up the motor, and began to drive toward town in the old truck. I was crossing the precipice into the big event. I was road-tripping this fifty-year-old piece of American steel from Oregon to Arizona over the next few days. I hadn't driven it for more than fifteen minutes up to this point and previous to that it sat under the walnut tree for twenty years.

I pulled up to Novak's, mouth watering for a delicious breakfast. Closed on Tuesdays. "Oh well, I'll just leave now," I decided. I grabbed a quick breakfast sandwich nearby and hit the road toward Lebanon, about twenty-five minutes away. Then I would drive through Sweet Home on my way to Bend...and then to the "desert of Oregon," according to Dwight. I hoped to make it to the Boise, Idaho, area before dark.

My dad held on to his F-250 for seventeen years after buying it brand new in late 1968. It was the truck he took my mom out for their first dates in. The truck he took out me to the forest to cut down Christmas trees in. I don't remember it all that well. He sold it when I was six years old to help facilitate the crazy idea. It helped my parents buy themselves the motorhome. The first family vehicle I remember well is that Jamboree. I remember sleeping in the bunk above the cab and crossing a long bridge in it during a torrential rainstorm. I remember the terror.

The next car of his I remember is a 1930 Model A.

After our motorhome adventure down the West Coast... when we arrived at my grandparent's place outside of Bisbee, Arizona...it was sitting front and center in the yard. Rust had eaten it's way through the door panels and covered every square inch. The interior was full of junk. The windshield was a spider web of broken glass. To me it was beyond repair. My dad was proud. He told me how he used to drive it when he was young. His uncle gave it to him in 1959. It was old back then.

Baby Andy with Grandpa and Grandma Littleton and the Model A
the way it sat out on the old homestead for years

By the time my dad took ownership it looked nothing like it used to. There were layers. Layers of paint under the rust. Layers of upholstery nailed on top of layers of sun-rotted upholstery. The rumble seat, one of the best features of the car, was gone. In it's place was a small truck bed. During World War II his uncle likely added the bed to get the red sticker that qualified him to buy more gas during Roosevelt's gas rationing. They sold little truck beds in the Sears & Roebuck catalogs.

My dad's assumption was that we would find a good place to find work and settle down within the next year or so. He told me about his dream to come back to get the Model A and fix it up. I loved the idea. Little did we know...all dreams would be on hold for quite some time. The Model A would spend many more years in Bisbee.

Our temporary move to Tucson of course, became permanent. My dad didn't find the good place to work. We lived in the Shady Haven. All plans to fix up old cars, or engage in meaningful artistic projects went by the wayside. My grandpa scrounged out an old light blue 70's Ford Pinto wagon from the Bisbee property and gave it to dad. It burned a lot of oil but got him back and forth to work. My mom called it the death-trap. Pinto's have unfortunate reputation for exploding when rear-ended.

My dad got all kinds of flack for the blue smoke plume he left behind him as he drove the Pinto around town. I remember riding with him as a kid. One time a guy yelled at us and gave him the finger. Dad smiled and waved at him. He looked over at me and said... "Hey, maybe that guy wants to help re-build the ole' engine. Should we ask him?" It made me smile.

For my mom, they found an old Chrysler Cordoba that ran fine but had no air conditioning and devoured gas. Being new to Tucson, the need for AC hadn't dawned on us yet. The massive steel car with burgundy interior would get red hot inside during the summer. Despite it's shortcomings, it got my mom to her new job at a high school library.

The one extra financial burden my mom and dad took on was to send me to private school. My mom had a master's degree and had taught at community colleges in Oregon. My dad had struggled in school, but realized how much his lack of credentials held him back. They decided to drive junky cars and buy second hand clothes to get their son a better education. I didn't realize what a sacrifice it was for them. Later on, my mom would tell me that she went ten years without buying herself new clothes.

All this time though, my dad and I would talk about the interesting old cars that we would see. He seemed to connect to machines. He grew up on the railroad and loved trains. He had a few sets of model trains he was saving for a future hobby room where he would set them up permanently. He always kept a look-out plastic toy cars and people. He planned to use them to create scenes for his trains to run through.

He would also subtly mourn the loss of the only brand new truck he had ever owned and that he loved so much. He had sacrificed it to help find a better life for his family, but that plan had failed. Now he was worse off financially, living in a city without any green trees to shade him on his walks, and he had given up his truck to get there. He wished that we could find our way into a better situation. He wanted to do some stuff for fun, like fixing up the old Model A...a project he had been dreaming of doing since he was fifteen years old.

We eventually got ourselves out of the Shady Haven. We met a guy at church who had property with mobile home spaces on it just outside of town. He gave us an incredible deal on rent. My parents would live there for the majority of the rest of their lives. They moved their old mobile home out there and eventually were able to upgrade to a newer and nicer one. They always took care of their things. We had one of the nicest trailers on the street by the time they finished it.

I helped build a shaded front porch and redo the kitchen and the floors. The new place and the low rent enabled my parents to have a little more available funds, especially after I left private school for public high school. My dad began to talk a little more about getting the old Model A from Bisbee before somebody else ended up with it.

In my early twenties, after I got home from a stint of schooling in Chicago, my mom encouraged me to help my dad go and get the Model A. My uncle helped extract it from among the other automotive carcasses in the desert surrounding the family home, and we towed it home to Tucson. My dad and I began to tear the car down and catalog the parts.

We planned to fully restore it ourselves until a good friend from Denver visited us and offered to help. He had experience restoring old Fords, so we took him up on it. In less than a year we had a shiny Model A sitting under the carport we built in preparation. It purred like a kitten and my dad was as excited as we had ever seen him. We would drive the old car around the neighborhood learning to adjust the fuel and the spark. He regularly cruised it down the dirt roads around the property they lived on. The neighbor's horse would gallop around its corral in excitement.

Fred Swanson and Dad with the restored Model A

We discovered though, as we attempted some longer drives, that driving a Model A is not for the faint of heart or for those in a hurry. The old car was prone to breaking down. I would later read in Ralph Moody's Shaking the Nickel Bush, the book my dad was hunting for when he met my mom in the bookstore in Lebanon, about a Model T that he and his travel companion bought and the litany of repair stops they had to make. It all made sense. My dad had read that too and was well aware of how unreliable these cars could be in their original state.

We loved to take the Model A around the neighborhood but longer adventures seemed like a headache in the making.

Once I promised to escort a couple from their wedding ceremony to their reception in the Model A. I created a 1930's outfit at a thrift store to wear as their chauffeur. My dad and I did all we could to make sure the old car was ready to roll. We had been having a little trouble so we consulted the old Model A expert in town. He taught me how to rebuild the carburetor and that seemed to do the trick. The day of the wedding though, it started to sputter and almost buck as I drove it down the street. I had to call and cancel on the couple at the last minute. We didn't want the newlyweds to get bucked out of the rumble seat. They rode in a Jaguar instead.

Around this time my dad concluded that, if we were going to take it very far, we would probably need to trailer it for the majority of the trip. His idea was to find an old F-250 like the one he had to give up to get the motorhome. It was always such a reliable truck for him. It would have plenty of power. My mom needed some down time from projects.

By this time my dad and mom had also found an old gutted-out Airstream trailer, another piece of Americana Dad always wished he could experience, in which he had begun to set up his model trains. He built risers and began laying out the track and setting up the scenes he had imagined so long ago on top of them. We decided to wait on the truck.

The year before Dad died we had begun to talk, every once in a while, about picking up an F-250 again. I showed him a listing for one like his, in blue, for sale in Tucson. He liked it. But we agreed that we needed to put away some cash before buying one was worth the thought. Not long after that he began to struggle with eating solid foods. Our concerns turned from finding an old truck to figuring out what was going on with him.

As I cruised in the old F-250 out of Lebanon my emotions swelled. I knew how much my dad would have loved the adventure I had been on. He would have loved the truck I found. He would have loved the time with me. I kept imagining the calm way in which he would have inhabited the passenger seat as we set out from one of the small towns toward the next. I saw him nodding with approval as I marveled at the beauty of the landscape. I played out the discussion he and I would have had about the truck. I would leave the rust. He would paint it like the one he used to have.

The old F-250 was running and was holding together for the time being, but there was a lot left to fix. The original white vinyl bench seat was disintegrating a little more every time I shifted my weight. It left my clothes dusted with foam particles each time I got out. The mirrors were mismatched and way too small. One of them was an ugly black plastic replacement that would smack flat against the door every time I accelerated onto the highway. I tried to use a piece of wire to hold in place to no avail. The original white plastic door panels were cracking and the chrome accents on the edges of them were peeling like snake skin. The antenna once snapped in the middle and now hung limp like a broken tree branch. The original radio was present but didn't make a sound. Who knows how many other mechanical parts were preparing to explode. After all, the truck had been sitting under a walnut tree, tail-end in a blackberry bush, for at least twenty years.

There was something about restoration that really resonated with my dad. When he could see the potential to restore something, he would advocate for just that. I wanted to rat-rod out the Model A, but he wanted it to look like a brand new car. He built with precision. When we were too poor to buy materials for home projects he would buy cull lumber and bend it back into shape. The finished product looked as good as if you had hired a handyman and bought the best materials.

I have a similar bent, but with a twist. I love to see an old thing repurposed too. I, in contrast, likely won't put a shiny perfect paint job on the F-250. I'll let the rust live on, but get it running like a dream and replace every missing part. I will absolutely figure out how to get the radio to work. I'm the type that finds a beautiful piece of old wood or steel and tries keep some of its characteristics of age while giving it a second life.

In a way, my dad had been given a second life as a young man in Oregon. He had set out to blaze a new trail for himself. He rejected his father's way of being a man, but he also failed in some of his endeavors. His new path had presented major bumps in the road. On it he discovered the darker sides of himself. He saw that he could get angry about the ways that life's not fair and that his choices could lead to real and negative consequences.

He also learned that forgiveness was real. He sensed that God was forgiving toward him despite his long list of failures. He saw that his wife and son loved him too. They were with him despite the ways he fell short of their expectations. Unfortunately my mom and I made him all too aware of his shortcomings throughout the years.

Amidst so many opportunities to give up, he seemed to keep within him a vision of life restored. He seemed to look back and look forward with some kind of expectation that the dreams of his heart weren't altogether lost. Somehow his favorite vehicles were an extension of those dreams. It wasn't just about the rusted heap of metal. The Model A was about his hopes. It was about seeing something everyone had given up on...restored to its former glory and enjoyed again.

For the meantime I was alone in the F-250, but somehow I sensed that my dad's dreams of restoration hadn't died. He's handed me the keys for now, but I believe his desire to see things made new again isn't his alone. For one, everyone I interacted with on my way home was excited to see my old truck back on the road with somebody who loves it in the driver's seat.

Why is it that so many people love to see restoration? I think it's a God-given longing of the soul. I think it points to something profoundly more permanent than old Fords. For now though, I get to taste the dream while driving an old piece of American steel.

I cruised well past Boise on day one, thanks to a lead foot, a strong 360 v8, and having missed out on that relaxing Hungarian breakfast I'd hoped for. I made it to a campground near Twin Falls, Idaho where I camped in the bed of the truck for the first time. I almost stopped earlier, due to a massive rainstorm on the horizon, but found nothing but seedy hotels in a town called Mountain Home. I decided to press on and found to my relief that the new wipers actually did function and that the lights all blazed bright. I arrived at the campground late. My phone was dead, so I found a couple with an RV who let me charge it off their electric while I slept. I crashed as soon as my body over-rode the discomfort of the truck bed and my mind blocked out the sounds of the campers next to me.

I awoke at daybreak. I quickly changed clothes and climbed in the cab. The truck fired right up, to my relief, and I set out on a mission to make it to Flagstaff on day two since I was ahead of schedule. I had decided to take the more scenic and less urban route to Arizona since the truck had no AC and was untested on the road. No AC in California sounded terrible, and Los Angeles with no AC and weak brakes sounded even worse.

I still had to get through Salt Lake City, Utah, though, which proved beyond stressful. I hit the city when traffic was bumper to bumper. The truck's brakes were functioning but feeling very weak. I decided to maintain a following distance of as-far-as-possible at all times. Downshifting became my best friend.

I was hungry, but hesitant to get into more big-city traffic off the freeway. The last lunch spot I spotted was in the town of Lehi where a KFC sign stood tall along the roadside and called my name. It turned out that this particular KFC used flour made at the local roller mill across the street.

This location's biscuits were noticeably superior. When my order came out late, an apologetic employee asked if they could get me anything to compensate. I was happy to be compensated with biscuits, and loaded up on them for the road. I wrapped the biscuits in the foil sandwich wrapper I had left over and set them up on the dashboard where the vent was always pumping in heat from the engine compartment. It turns out that the heater switch was stuck. I covered them with my thrifted Lebanon High School baseball cap. The result; I was back on the road with piping hot biscuits on hand all day long.

I was in for quite a treat as I traveled through southern Utah. I deviated from the main freeway system and took the small curvy roads through the national forests and national parks between Provo and Page, my first planned stop in Arizona. I crept up and down mountain roads, continually impressed at the F-250's ability to handle the inclines. The declines were a little more dicey.

Two things were beginning to register in my mind. First, the motor was getting increasingly loud. It seemed like it was running fine, but the tractor-on-the-run sounds were re-emerging. And second, the brakes were not doing the job. I knew all along that the truck did not have power brakes, but this was beyond non-power status. The only vehicle I had driven without power brakes was the Model A. On it, the brakes are entirely manual...meaning your foot pressure is the operative pressure system causing the vehicle to stop.

I reasoned that this truck was just old and, therefore, the brakes weren't meant so much for highways as for farms and small towns. I honed the art of downshifting. I gave people plenty of space. I was especially aware of the brakes as I drove from Page to Flagstaff, Arizona. I descended a beautiful canyon, but could hardly focus on the scenery. My main goal was to not die, and the possibilities of death loomed at every hairpin curve. Steep cliffs and blind corners confronted me.

The people ahead gave no thought to the condition of the rusty old truck in their rearview.

I made it though, and rolled into Flagstaff around 9:30 p.m. Unfortunately I arrived too late to check into the campground I had looked up during my lunch break. I stopped to fuel up and re-formulate my plan.

While I pumped gas an incredibly drunk man stumbled over and up to the truck positioning himself about three inches from my face. He began to reason with me as to how I might be of service to him. I was exhausted, worried about the brakes, and unsure of where I was going to sleep. He began to touch me on the shoulder over and over and appeared increasingly agitated as I evaded his specific requests.

I said... "Hey, I have an idea! Follow me over here." I took off walking toward the attached convenience store. He followed me, a little thrown off I'm sure. I told him, "Wait here for a minute," and I walked back to the truck, fired it up, and threw it in gear. My plan became clear. I decided right then and there that I was going to drive through the night and get home to my family. Sleep would have to wait.

I stopped about thirty minutes later and bought myself an Arnold Palmer flavored energy drink. I never drink those things but figured this might be the moment they were designed for. It turned out to be a great decision. It tasted nothing like tea or lemonade...more like medicine. But it kicked in somewhere around Camp Verde and I rode the energy wave all the way home.

The next big city I hit was Phoenix, and I barreled through a little after midnight. The freeways are usually abuzz but I nearly had the road to myself. The midnight summer air hovered around 90 degrees. It's strange to be sweating while driving at night but it sure beats driving in the blazing Arizona sun in a glass and steel box. I knew I had made the right decision by driving all night. As I left the big city the air began to cool and relax me as it whipped through the cab. Two hours later I was home to my family. The old truck had made it and I was beyond relieved. I didn't die and now I would drift off to sleep in my own bed a day early.

Later weeks would reveal that all but one of the brake shoes had frozen up either before or during my trip. I drove from Oregon to Arizona with half of one fifty-year-old drum brake to slow me down. On top of that I discovered the unfinished work of the mechanic back in Albany. The brand new manifold gaskets disintegrated due to the highly pressurized air leaking through the gaps. I was low on oil. Against all odds, both myself and the truck were safe and sound.

Back at home I thanked God for keeping me safe on the road. Poor decisions can lead to real failures, and this could have been one of mine.

Thankfully, I got a second chance to tell my story. The old truck's engine was fine and restoration continues. My restoration continues as well.

I hope my dad somehow gets to know that his son is carrying on his dream of seeing old things made new. I hope that someday we will reflect on it all together...however that works. God only knows.

4

Love

Leroy, the man of few words, could also get himself into quite the long conversation. He and Bud, a neighbor we had for a number of my high school and young adult years, could stand out in front of the mobile homes and talk for hours...at least that's how long it seemed to me.

My mom used to go outside and break it up. She would call him inside with "Supper's getting cold", or something like that. Of course, the supper often consisted of sliced deli turkey, veggies, and some dip on a plate...all ideally served cold, but the very idea of a meal just sitting there on the table wasting away was enough to make any man walk away from a fellow conversationalist mid-sentence.

When it clearly wasn't suppertime, she'd bluntly inform Bud that he needed to go home. She didn't like how he came over and talked politics and about everything going wrong in the world. He drove her "up a wall."

It wasn't all Bud's fault though...oh no...Leroy had a way of keeping a conversation moving himself. This was especially true over the right topic. There were certain categories such as fair pay, or "eatin' right", or even politics that he could get into on the right day. He'd have a thing or two to say. But he also did a good job of letting the other guy drawl on about his point of view if he so desired. Then he'd pitch in an "Ah, I don't know about that..." which the other party inevitably interpreted as an invitation to respond with a new diatribe. The end result though, was that the people, who got the chance, tended to like their talks with him.

As a kid, my dad subjected me to utter torture. We would be out somewhere...let's say the hardware store, and the guy that worked there showed himself a talker. Well, if he was talking, then my dad was all in. He'd hang out, cross his arms casually, and not appear to be looking for a way out of it. He'd egg the conversation on and show interest. He would even encourage him!

And there I'd be, bored out of my mind, sitting down on a lower shelf...playing with a miniature pipe-wrench shaped cigarette lighter that had suddenly become the best entertainment option I had. It wasn't uncommon for our thirty-minute errand to take well over an hour under the guidance of Leroy the conversationalist.

It would seem, now, that I've inherited my father's propensity to get myself into long conversations. Trouble is...I am not the man of few words he was. My poor daughter has to stand and sit around while I shoot the breeze back and forth about topics she couldn't care less about. Politics, religion, furniture design, some interesting tale of adventure I just have to share...all are fair game. Just ask her...it's utter torture, especially when she has to spend full days with me during summer break.

One day in Bisbee I went into Bathtub Coffee, a new place on the scene at the time, to get some writing done. I had been parked at a table for twenty minutes or so when a couple of older guys walked in. One of them was blind and needed some help to get situated on the bench next to me. He got set up and I got back to writing.

After a bit I noticed the other guy removing a didgeridoo out of a long black bag he had carried in with him. He extended it out toward the bench I was sitting on next to the blind guy and placed the end of it between us on the bench. Then he began to blow into it. This did not go unnoticed by myself or anyone else in the coffee shop. If you've experienced the playing of a didgeridoo in person, this will be of no surprise to you. I was supposed to be focusing on my writing, but I couldn't help myself.

"Hey, nice didge man!" I offered.

"Thanks. Yeah, I've got a few. Got one made out of a tree branch. You're not supposed to...but I got two drill bits and just drilled it out. I've got a nice one made out of bamboo, too."

"Agh, cool...I've got one made of Eucalyptus I got in Australia...the kind that's hollowed out naturally by termites." It's true, I did.

"Want to sell it?" he asked.

"Maybe...I'll have to think about that..."

Now, I'll spare you. Because this was the beginning of at least an hour's talk. I learned his name was Mike, and the blind guy was a friend he was catching up with named Greg.

Somehow we went from didgeridoos straight into religion. Now, that's quite a feat. Usually it takes more steps than that. Religion segued quickly into politics, which led us into some fascinating discussion about life after death, consciousness, near death experiences, then somehow back to politics and finally back to the didgeridoo.

I remembered that I needed to sell something to get a part for the old F-250 without breaking the bank. I had stumbled upon just the part I needed the day before. I told Mike he might have caught me at the perfect time to sell my didge. I made sure to get his phone number so we could arrange a meet up for him and the didge. Mike seemed excited by his new opportunity though a little distracted. He kept getting up from the table and walking around. Poor Greg would keep chatting away to the empty chair in front of him.

Quick note...Greg asks that you please let blind people know when you're leaving the area. You know...they can't see that you're no longer there.

I then helped Greg navigate out of the restroom before I had to go. Mike and I agreed to check in a couple days later when I could bring the didgeridoo to town, and Greg called out, "I hope I get to visit with you again!"

I've learned from my dad that just taking the time to talk and, especially listen to people, is hardly ever a waste of time. It's inefficient, I know, but not a waste of time. Why's that? Because people are not a waste of time. They have all kinds of weird views on things (and by the way, they say the same thing about you...which is something my dad would have said), but they are people all the same and well worth a little time to get to know. Sometimes you even find yourself with a friend, or at least a good acquaintance.

An unexpected surprise awaited me in Bisbee on my second trip. It was finding that part I needed for the old F-250. I found it on my commute up to Old Bisbee from my friend Jesse's house in Naco. I had to leave the truck at home because it was having some little issues, but it had one more major issue I had been keeping my eye on.

The radiator support panel, that also tied the two fenders together and to the frame in the front, was rusty when I got the truck in Oregon. By the time I got home and had done a trip or two, one of which included me nailing a curb on a failed U-turn, the old piece of steel was officially collapsing. It seemed the truck was holding together up front, but there was a noticeable sag on the front right side.

Buying a new radiator support was not fitting into my

budget after I'd done my traveling for the year. I knew my only shot at getting it done anytime soon was to find the part used and swap it myself. I wasn't quite sure where to start, considering the age of the truck.

Every day, when I would drive up to write in Bisbee, I would pass an auto repair shop that had a bunch of older vehicles sitting around on the surrounding lot. I guessed that most of them had come from the area. Arizona cars don't tend to have the cancerous rust that vehicles from colder and wetter climates do.

The first time I saw the place, I had a feeling I should stop in, but I talked myself out of it for the first four days of my trip. On the fifth day I was running ahead of schedule for something and was right by the shop, so I went for it. As I walked up to the front an old mechanic came walking out...

"Can I help you?"

"Hey...uh...I'm just looking for an old 68 Ford...uh...you know, the radiator support for a F-250...68." I stammered out.

"You know...I'm not a wreckin' yard." He answered, walking back into his shop."

"Oh, yeah I know, sorry. I just saw you had a lot of older stuff around."

He looked back over his shoulder with a slight grin. "I think I got what you need."

He walked me out back to one of his parts trucks. Sure enough, there was a 68 F-100 Ranger; same body and trim style. The radiator support was in great shape, no wrecks no rust. It had paperwork in the glove box proving it an Arizona truck, originally purchased in Scottsdale. It even looked to me as if it had the one piece of chrome trim mine was missing. I was so glad I stopped!

The mechanic told me he would give me a good price, but he didn't have time to pull it himself. That was no problem; I kind of needed the practice since I planned to re-install it on my truck.

As we walked back, he began telling me why he had the

parts truck. He had it because he had a rare four-door F-250 that needed a motor. Then he showed me an old 50's Ford flatbed he'd been working on. Finally he mentioned a T-Bird.

He paused a moment and then invited me over behind a closed-off portion of his shop. The whole shop was fairly cluttered with miscellaneous parts, but this room was clean… and inside it was an incredible black Thunderbird! "This one's not even my nice one," he smiled. My dad loved T-Bird's, so as a result, I always have, too. This one was a beauty.

"If you come back to get that part next week, maybe I'll bring the other one over," he offered.

"Oh, I'd love that! This is a beautiful car!" I exclaimed. He smiled.

These were the types of interactions I always had with my dad. He had a knack for getting people to share what they loved with him and show him their cool stuff. Rarely did he ask. He would just listen to them as they began to share with him, and they would gradually decide they could trust him with more. Often a newly-made friend would give him an interesting item to take home or invite him over to see something very special to them. People could tell he was genuinely interested in them, even though he often offered far fewer words in the conversation.

Days later, when I came back to pull the radiator support, I actually showed up with Mike, the guy who was playing the didgeridoo at the coffee shop. I had seen him again and decided to offer him money toward the didge if he would help me get the work done. Two sets of hands are always better than one on projects like this.

As we crawled around in the dirt getting all the old bolts off, Mike told me a lot about himself. He'd had a really interesting life. He had traveled widely, and seemed to have found ways to make enough money doing simple handyman and craftsman type jobs to keep himself moving. We talked music, religion, old cars, and a little politics, of course. We were a great team and got the radiator support. plus a couple other parts I spotted, off in just a few hours.

When I took him back to the coffee shop in town, he said I should give him a call the next time I came to town. I'm looking forward to it.

Mike with the radiator support at the auto shop in South Bisbee

---

On my first day on the Amtrak train to Oregon, as we meandered the hills of California, they called my name to come have dinner in the dining car. I hadn't ridden the Amtrak since I went on a trip with my mom as a kid, so I really had no idea what to expect.

As I walked through the train cars ahead of me, being jostled back and forth as the train was moving at a fairly quick pace, I was behind a lady who seemed to be headed the same way. We reached the dining car together and, after giving our names, were both called to follow the stewardess. To our surprise, she sat us at the table with two other gentlemen. So here we were, four strangers staring at one another across the table settings. We had to talk.

The lady jumped right into conversation by asking if we were all there on business. The gentleman to her left briefly replied "yes", and hearing nothing more, she moved to the gentleman across from him.

He was a slightly disheveled but well-spoken man, three quarters bald with enough hair dangling over the shoulders to make up for it. He wore a floral-print button-down shirt, the type you really ought to iron, at least between the buttons, so as to avoid peepholes, but he hadn't done so. His peepholes were fully functioning.

He began by stating that he'd been walking a trail from the US / Mexico border to Canada, which immediately intrigued the table. Why do such a thing? Why did you just board this train in California instead of finishing?

He shared that he had made it well over two hundred miles and then heard from his landlord in the Pacific Northwest that she would be moving, which meant he had to move and move now. He had an option however, one he seemed quite excited about, which was to drive her car to Pittsburg for her.

His new plan consisted of driving her sweet Mazda to Pittsburg, then jumping back onto the Amtrak from there back to California. This trip was reportedly a 90-hour ride (making my sense of tedium on the first day of our 30-hour ride seem quite silly), upon the completion of which he planned to re-engage with his trek from Mexico to Canada. The only downside to the complete derailing of his plan, that he could identify, was the technicality that he would be homeless in a couple days.

A thousand other questions came to my mind, but the lady was more intrigued and eager than I. She jumped back in with questions about the dangers of the trail, such as wild animals.

He promptly replied that her concern was not misguided.

In fact, such dangers were most definitely present and he had even experienced them himself.

On a previous journey he had agreed to walk alone overnight in order to deliver a backpack full of raw meat that someone needed transported before it went bad. On this trek he had distinctly heard, several times, what sounded like people chatting around the next bend of the trail, but each time he would round the bend he found that the sounds were coming from the opposite direction of the trail's turn, and that they now were coming from still further ahead.

He confidently asserted that these voices were none other than the alluring call of a cougar, which had learned to mimic the human voice as it sounded from a short distance and was seeking to trap him in order to get to his backpack full of raw meat (and I suppose the raw meat on his own bones). Fortunately, however, he had steadfastly stuck to his mission and completed the journey without incident. He delivered the meat before it spoiled and lived to tell the tale.

The lady had a stunned look on her face and asked,

"Now is that your opinion or do cougars actually do that?"

I was wondering the same. All of a sudden, though, she doubled back recollecting a similar experience of her own in which she had visited a friend's house where she heard haunting voices in the night. She had eventually discovered that the voices were coming from the dog as it slept. This dog, she asserted, mumbled in human language in its sleep on a regular basis.

The two of them continued to discuss all of this as the businessman and I gave each other understanding glances of amusement and doubt. This all went on until the businessman, who had clearly paid more for the train ride than the rest of us, was invited to leave the table without paying for his meal by the stewardess.

Now there were three, and the lady continued to press the gentleman next to me for more tales of adventure and for the "why" behind his free-spirited lifestyle.

He volunteered that he suffered from a disorder and her interest only increased. She reported that she suffered from the same malady. She pressed him to explain more and he vaguely referred to some bad things that once happened to him. He then went on to clarify that all of the traveling and the walking helped him on his journey to understand himself.

His conclusion was that what all people generally need is for someone to be nice to them even if they don't understand them. People didn't always understand him, he said, because he did things that "didn't need to mean anything" from time to time. Why did he do them? He didn't know. We might have noticed, he mentioned, that he had a tail.

In fact, we had NOT noticed, as we were all seated at a dining table. Nor did we fully comprehend the words that were coming out of his mouth. He went on.

Apparently some time ago on the trails he had split his shorts and hadn't noticed it for a number of days. He discovered his newly-formed peephole via the discovery of sand in his blanket that he'd picked up every time he sat down during his travels. Then he inadvertently deposited the sand into his blanket from the split in his pants every time he lay down.

Another trail walker asked him if he wanted help fixing his shorts and he replied that what he really wanted was a ttail, for which the current state of his shorts would be well suited.

It just so happened that one of his hiking companions, previously unbeknownst to him, engaged in the tail business herself. In fact, she regularly produced high quality tails for people to wear, and there was a real market for such a thing. I've confirmed that this is true.

Said companion made a slight detour over to a thrift store in the area and found a small rug of significant nap, which when folded and sewed in half, looked just like the type of tail her buddy could sport. It all got sewed together with the addition of some wire to give a bit of lift, and voila...he had a tail and the split in his shorts had meaning.

The lady and I were enthralled with this story, especially

since amidst the telling of it, the gentleman had gently lifted the tail out from under himself and had presented it there before us on the dining car table. We found the veracity of the story much more reasonable by this exhibition. By extension I accepted the veracity of his other tales.

He said people on the trails called him Strange Bird, and that he was somewhat well known as "that guy with the tail." I suppose that must be true. The time had come to head back to our respective seats. I had loved every minute of my lunchtime. Strange Bird walked by my seat on the way to his. His tail had perfect lift and looked quite convincing.

Strange Bird shared that he has made many great friends on his journeys but that many people also disdain him. He explained that people either find him interesting, or they seem to have no time for him. I find myself incredibly intrigued by, and comfortable with, guys like him. I know why. I learned it from my dad.

I didn't really tell my story at the lunch table that day. I threw out my occupation and destination when asked at one point, but most of that lunch time belonged to Strange Bird.

My dad was the master of being the listening ear. If someone had wild tales of adventure to tell, he was quite happy to let them tell all. He was never bothered when someone else took up the time and presented themselves as more interesting.

In fact, my dad seemed to gravitate to the odd ones out, and folks of the category seemed to deeply esteem him. I remember a few of the employees of the lumber yard where my dad worked when I was a kid, but the one who stood out was Spike.

Spike was always full of tales and full of energy as I remember. One of the few days I went to work with my dad, I remember Spike hootin' and hollerin' as he sped through the lumber yard on his moped.

In my twenties I ended up living down the street from Spike's mobile home. He seemed a master of repurposed yard decor. A feature at Spike's place was his carport roof that faced the street. He had it lined with rusty Tonka trucks, his very own fleet of heavy equipment. I bet he and Strange Bird would have gotten along, and I bet Spike would have worn a tail if somebody'd made him one.

Following my dad through life, I learned to be comfortable with folks like Spike and Strange Bird. Not only to be comfortable with them, but to genuinely enjoy their presence and their antics. My dad would always lovingly give his attention to guys like Spike, and show genuine care about their well-being.

I doubt I'll see Strange Bird again, but I won't have to look far to find folks cut from the same cloth. In fact, I should probably go check on "ole' Spikey" as my dad would call him. The lumber yard is long gone, now turned into an upscale restaurant, but there's a Tonka truck-lined carport facing the street in my old neighborhood, and I bet Spike's still there.

About a year later I spotted Spike in his yard. I stopped
and we chatted for a while. He's looking for more Tonka
trucks if anybody's got some they aren't holding on to.

5
Sacrifice

"Do unto others as you would have them do unto you."
A lot of wise people, including Jesus of Nazareth

My trip to small town Oregon began with a day in Los Angeles. The original plan was to merely pass through the city on the train I would catch in Tucson. But when I learned the train ride from Tucson to L.A. took at least ten hours, ran overnight, and cost a lot more than a plane ticket for a one-hour flight I adjusted my plan. My best flight option landed me in L.A. just under a day early. This meant my small-town trip commenced with me finding my way around my dad's least favorite city to navigate. I booked the cheapest room I could find that was as close to the train station as possible. I wanted to be in and out.

At first I dreaded the day. I envisioned finding my way across the city with all my luggage and then sitting around with nothing to do. That all changed when I talked to my buddy Matt. Matt used to be in a middle school group I directed at a church in Tucson, and we have kept in touch ever since. He reminded me that his college wasn't too far from the L.A. airport. He happened to be free for the day, willing to pick me up, and wanted to grab breakfast and go thrift store shopping. All of that...music to my ears.

We started off our day together eating at John O'Groats, where Jerry Seinfeld and Larry David got breakfast in Comedians in Cars Getting Coffee, and found a couple of decent thrift spots. The best one was the Goodwill in Beverly Hills.

As we left the Goodwill with a couple of new additions to our wardrobes, Matt threw out the idea that I could hang out with him and his friend Maria for the rest of the afternoon. I was all for it. My only other plan was sitting in the bedroom I had reserved in someone else's house. The renter had supplied the disclaimer that he had a lot of roommates. I had no desire to do anything besides sleep there for the night. On the way to meet Maria, Matt informed me that the two of them were about to be on a date. I offered to bail but he said it sounded fun to bring me along.

The date turned out to be quite the event, much to our surprise. We went to an amazing bookstore in downtown L.A., and that's where Matt's master plan fell apart. He had found the most incredible parking spot right in front of the store, street-side. We went in and began to explore. I grabbed an old book on ranch-style furniture design and found a seat. Matt and Maria went to browse the aisles and each other's souls.

Maria casually checked in to see if Matt had fed his meter. He glanced down at his watch only to discover he had transgressed by fifteen minutes. Unconcerned, he strolled outside. The car had disappeared! It was as if the tow company had targeted his vehicle, parked next to it, and towed it the moment the meter expired. Matt called right away and it was already in the impound yard at least ten minutes away.

Fortunately Maria had a car we could take to track his down. It was a rental that she was nervous to drive but it got us through the jam-packed streets. Between finding the lot, standing in line with angry urbanites, proving that Matt's dad was the owner of the vehicle, and actually extracting the SUV from the crowded lot, we invested a good two hours of date time into the situation. The best part is...I think Maria had a blast and I bet neither of them will ever forget the date.

Back on the road, they helped me find my rental room and we tried out a Vietnamese restaurant down the street. I thanked them for letting me tag along. I couldn't have planned a more entertaining day.

On our way to dinner something dawned on me. My rental spot sat at the foot of a very familiar hill. I had noticed, when I'd looked at the map while booking the room, that my room wasn't too far from Dodger Stadium. What I hadn't grasped was how close. Dodger Stadium is somewhat atop a small hill in the city, and I managed to book myself right at the hill's base. I could take an easy stroll right up to the stadium. Were the Dodgers in town that night? I saw some non-descript event signs as we walked back toward my room. I began to get my hopes up.

Matt and Maria headed out and I checked in to my room. Sure enough, there were a lot of roommates and the place wasn't what I would call clean. Wine bottles were strewn throughout the living room. The guy that met me there pitched the availability of wine as a perk. It seemed like someone regularly slept on the couch. I checked the schedule online and indeed...the Dodgers were hosting the Cincinnati Reds.

I sat in my room for about five minutes and decided I had little to lose. The roads were dark, but I didn't need to get too far. I lived in South Chicago for a bit, so I know how to keep my head down and fade into urban terrain. By the time I had worked through all this in my mind I was already out the door and walking up a grassy hill toward the stadium. I had to see some baseball.

You see, I loved baseball as a kid. I lived and breathed it. I played baseball, I watched baseball, I collected baseball cards, my favorite movie is still Field of Dreams. I was a baseball kid through and through.

My dad though, not so much. My dad wasn't a sports guy at all. He never played sports. He never watched sports. Sports were nowhere on his radar, but you would never have known that if you'd have observed my family when I was a kid. How so? My parents decided that since I was into sports, they'd give it a go themselves.

My dad frequented not only my baseball games. He also took me to innumerable Tucson Toros (once the triple-A team for the Houston Astros) games and Major League Spring Training games. Most of the games we went to followed long days at work for him. To involve himself in my favorite pastime even more, he even collected baseball cards. He declared Nolan Ryan his favorite player and bought a card or two of his whenever he took me to a card show. Family friends of ours had sold Nolan Ryan their home in California, which influenced his choice to be a fan. Dad thought it was cool that he had stayed in the night in the great Nolan Ryan's house!

Back then I thought this all to be completely reasonable. "Of course Dad would do these things. The only reason he didn't do them before I came along was that he hadn't been exposed to their amazingness." I didn't see that he was doing them for me.

Another thing our family did, that became a feature of our out-of-town trips, was going to Major League stadiums and games. We didn't travel too much, but we got to Coors Field in Denver during the Colorado Rockies Inaugural season. To this day I recollect a fly getting inside of my ear and biting me at that game. My own wife doesn't believe it happened, but I trust you do.

One year we went to California to go to SeaWorld and Disneyland. I really wanted to see a Major League game. Watching the Angels play in Anaheim would have been far more convenient, but the Dodgers were a much more iconic team, and I wanted to experience Dodger Stadium.

We braved the L.A. traffic, which my dad hated more than anything. We paid for parking at the stadium. We walked a long way up to the ticket booth. We bought what I assumed were the cheapest tickets we could get...out in the outfield bleachers. I didn't care about the cheap seats though. I was at a Dodgers game! Mom and Dad got me a New Era fitted Dodgers hat. We took pictures to prove it all happened to anyone who may have disbelieved that I had been to Dodger Stadium. To top it all off, I chased down a home run ball that came crashing into the bleachers. It was an amazing day for the young Andy Littleton.

Having shaped the bill of my brand new hat, I was ready for some baseball at Dodger Stadium.

As 35-year-old Andy walked up the same hill toward Dodger Stadium, some things began to sink in. I thought about all the time my family, and especially my dad, devoted to baseball. Once I stopped playing, he stopped watching games or collecting cards. Obviously he hadn't discovered his new favorite thing when he had embraced baseball. He did it all for me.

As I walked up to the fence surrounding the stadium, I was shocked to see that people were spending $30-$50 just to park. I approached the ticket counter and asked the sweet elderly lady behind the glass for the cheapest ticket they had. She pointed to her stadium map and said those seats were way up in the decks above right field. I expected her to point to the outfield bleachers, but they were a good deal more expensive.

Climbing toward my cheap seat, I paused at a stand selling Dodgers gear. New Era fitted caps were still for sale, and they were the most expensive option. I know my parents had a very limited budget. I realized that they scraped the bottom of the barrel to give their middle school boy the time of his life at Dodger Stadium. As I took my seat high in the upper deck, where the players looked like ants below, the amount of sacrifice my parents made to support my hobby dawned on me.

I realized that my dad's sacrifice, for the sake of his son and baseball, was especially incredible. He was un-athletic to say the least, and very embarrassed of it. Yet he would play catch with me time and time again amidst my complaining about his throws being off the mark. He came to every Little League match of mine he could. He attended dozens and dozens of professional games.

Dad worked long hours at the lumberyard, including a lot of overtime, yet he would make sure to take me out to the ballgames happening in town. He would get us there early, so I could chase down former major leaguers for their autographs during warm ups. He usually stayed deep into the night as I tried to catch players walking from the locker rooms to their cars after the game. Sometimes he brought his star-struck kid home past midnight, because a player I believed was an up-and-coming star was in town.

These were unforgettable experiences for me. Between the minor league teams that played all season and the major league teams that came through in the spring, I got hundreds of autographs. With my dad's help I got to meet players as well known as Ryne Sandberg of the Chicago Cubs, Tony Gwynn of the San Diego Padres, and Alex Rodriguez who played Triple-A ball in the Seattle Mariners system before becoming a superstar on the New York Yankees. It was an amazing time in my life.

I never asked my dad if doing all of that was hard for him,

but I know it must have been a sacrifice. On top of the games and TV time watching baseball at home, he also took me to card shows where I "invested" my money into baseball cards and memorabilia. Of course, my money was money I "earned" from my parents, and they never counted up the time and travel costs and charged them to me.

Not only was a lot of time and money sacrificed, but a lot of mental and emotional energy was also given to something that wasn't of any personal interest to my dad at all. I was his interest in it all. He wanted to know me, understand me, and be with me. He would sacrifice whatever he could to make that possible.

On that first day of my journey to Oregon, I was struck by the importance of such sacrifice. The streets of L.A. are flooded with people who suffer with disorders and need care. Many turned to drugs or alcohol, at some point, to their detriment.

When Matt, Maria and I were heading to the impound yard, we drove through skid row. It was a sobering sight. I wonder what these people's dads were like. What if someone in their family wanted to know them enough to sacrifice the things they'd like to be doing to invest in them? What if anybody did? Would that change anything? Could it have... back in their childhood?

At the Dodgers game a young mentally handicapped boy was with, who I assume to have been, a family member. They didn't speak as father and son, but they had the familiarity you would expect between uncle and nephew. They, like me, had bought the cheapest tickets. They, like me, walked down to the lower levels to stand and watch the game up close.

Working with this kid looked like it took a lot of patience, but his uncle (we'll assume) took it in stride. He said they had come to two games so far this year. The kid was decked out in Dodgers gear and was having the time of his life. The stadium security guy gave him a "#1 Fan" button to add to his outfit.

I'm sure his uncle could have been doing a hundred other things with his evening. He had none of his friends around, and he was out late on a weeknight. No doubt he'd had a long week of work so far. He could have stayed home to recoup, went out for a beer with the guys…the list could go on. But instead he gave the night to this kid, and it sounded like it was a regular event for the two of them. I doubt this kid ends up on the L.A. streets like so many other mentally handicapped folks who grow up there do. Why? Because he has someone willing to sacrifice to take care of him.

I had that too. I grew up in a trailer park in Tucson during my early years. Many kids who grow up there, end up there. All too often they end up in a worse situation than the parents that raised them.

But my life was different. My dad taught me that some of the most incredible gifts are given at great personal cost. They often aren't even the gifts we understand. A life of sacrifice lived for the care and benefit of others is beautiful, no matter how much material wealth you have to pull from. I'm sure my dad had to learn this over time, and he dropped the ball an awful lot of times. But I see a theme of sacrifice in my dad's life that made a huge impact on a kid who loved baseball so much that he thought going to a game at Dodger Stadium was as good as it gets.

Of course, the sacrificial life isn't only found in the big events, the baseball games and out-of-town trips of life.

On my fourth day in Albany I found myself ready to move on. The F-250 was so close to ready to drive, but the master cylinder we got from the auto parts store had a defect and getting another one in from Portland would take a full day. We had ordered it the night before but hours stood between the breakfast I was eating and go-time. My options were to sit around at Dwight's place for the day or make a move.

I asked Dwight if he wanted to drive me around the area, but he needed to get some work done on the farm. He was willing to get me into town to pick up the master cylinder, so we negotiated that he would take me in early.

I decided I might as well rent a car so I could be more mobile for the day, which pained me. It was for the best though. It allowed me to get to Lebanon for the day while the truck was immobile. In fact, I ended up needing it a few more days, once my plan shifted to getting the exhaust guy involved.

As Dwight and I prepared to leave, I got a call from the rental agency that the car I was supposed to get wasn't there yet. I told Dwight to take me anyway. I kind of wanted to go thrift store shopping.

OK, the truth is, I really wanted to go thrift store shopping. I always do. I love finding vintage local items, made in USA clothes, knick-knacks, and furniture we can restore back home. At this point I also wanted to piece together that little tool kit to keep with me in the truck. It seemed like the least I should do since we had tweaked so many things on the truck in my first two days of ownership.

My first stop was St. Vinny's, the Catholic thrift store in town. It turned out to be a great one! It was surprisingly organized and had a ton of inventory. I got a couple of good books to take home, a nice long sleeved and made in USA shirt, and a solid collection of tools.

On top of all that I found a Pro-Stock Louisville Slugger baseball bat for only $7. A Pro-Stock was the kind of bat I saw the big leaguers using when I went to games as a kid. I liked it no matter what, but I also figured that on a week's journey by myself, it wouldn't be the worst thing in the world to have in the truck. When I got back I mounted it on the F-250's seat-back gun rack.

Thrifting is an interesting hobby for me. My parents didn't do as much of it as they used to in my later years. It had moved from necessity to hobby, from the only place we could get clothes or furniture, to an option we could consider. You wouldn't find any thrift store clothes in my dad's closet in his later years.

Thrifted clothes are nearly all I buy. As a kid we got kind of stuck in Tucson, and the only place we could afford to shop at that point was the thrift store. I lied about it to my friends at school, and my parents kind of kept it under wraps. For some reason when I got older I decided, after a stint of blowing all my money on new clothes in high school, that thrift store shopping was the way to go. Now it's essentially my favorite sport. I love finding high-quality stuff at a great price.

I didn't expect to have my memory jogged on the way out of the thrift store though. I had loaded up my backpack with my treasures and set off for the rental car agency. As I walked through the parking lot, I saw a screw on the ground and instinctively picked it up and relocated it under a tree where it couldn't puncture anyone's tire.

Immediately it dawned on me...I always do that. Dad always did that. There was no question in his mind. If something like that could be done to help other people out, he would do it. He never explained that to me or gave me a lecture about how I should do such things. In fact, when in a hurry I'd sometimes protest. But he would quietly do it and say something like "Oh, it only takes a second."

He would also return, not only our grocery cart...but any grocery cart near our vehicle...to the cart corral when we went to the grocery or hardware store. Again, no lecture. No explanation. I don't know when I began to do it too instead of just watching him, but at some point I did. Later in his life we would even return carts together without ever communicating the plan. Sometimes I would even try to beat him to a cart and just smile at him.

Somewhere along the way I realized why my dad did that. He never worked at a supermarket, but he did work at a lumberyard with carts the customers used. A lot of people undoubtedly took the carts way out to their trucks in the parking lot and left them out there. My dad and the other "yard dogs" would have to chase them down amidst all of their other work. I assume my dad had also gotten a screw or two stuck in his tire throughout his life.

His logic was simple. "I wish a few more customers had brought those carts back to the yard for us...so I'll do that for the people here at the grocery store." "I wish somebody'd picked up that screw that got in my tire and left me stuck out on the road...so I'll toss any screw I see layin' around off the road so it doesn't happen to somebody else."

My dad never lectured me on these things, but he taught me well to "do unto others as you would have them do unto you." I'm sure he did more of those things than I was aware of. I'm sure he applied the principle to more and more situations as he journeyed through life. Before I realized he had taught me any of this, I started similar practices of my own.

I worked in food service during high school. It was difficult to bus the table when people left their dirty dishes sitting right in front of them, like they were kings, or pushed them to the center of the table. When I came by I would have to stretch to pick them up while balancing the ones I had in hand. Inevitably, when overloaded with a tray of dishes, someone would call me over and ask me to reach in front of them or to the center of the table to take one more saucer that was encroaching on their space.

It was my job to clear the tables, but this always felt a little un-thoughtful. I think everyone should be a server for at least a month if they plan to eat out the rest of their life. Every once in awhile, a patron would stack their dishes nicely on the corner of the table for us servers and bus-boys. I always appreciated that so much. It showed me that this person was thinking of the staff and wanted to make our jobs a little bit easier.

Around that time in my life I started stacking my dishes for the wait staff when I went out to eat. It's not a hard thing to do, and your server will feel a little bit more cared for. I'm sure it will come as no surprise when I tell you that your service often gets a little quicker too. I wonder how much of that decision came from having a dad who did such sacrificial things subtly, teaching me to the same throughout my life.

Without ever speaking the words he taught to "do unto others as you would have them do unto you."

6
Patience

On my last full day in Lebanon, just before I'd pick up the old Ford and hit the road back home, I sat in Lebanon at the Korner Kitchen. I sipped a nice warm cup of coffee from the perfect-sized mug, read the morning paper, and contemplated where to go after breakfast. Under the table I systematically stretched my legs, feet and toes. I was feeling the walks I had been taking and feeling them bad. I had done a workday's worth of walking over the weekend.

My first walk was about five hours down the beautiful Oregon Coast on Saturday. I wore a pair of sandals that were great quality and all but, unfortunately, my feet weren't aware of that fact and didn't care. I now had significant red-as-if-sanded-down rings around my big toes and an irritating itch to go with them. On top of the pain and itch, my legs were just downright tired. I love to walk and like to think I walk a lot, but I hadn't done anything like a five-hour trek in some time.

The next day was Sunday and I went to church at Lebanon First Assembly in the morning. There I hoped to track down the old addresses where my family lived from a church directory and experience the church I spent my early years attending.

Folks there were busy getting ready for the service when I arrived, but they stopped what they were doing to greet a new young guy. When I shared that I grew up at the church the greeter said to wait while he found Penny for me. Penny was a sweet lady who had been around the church a long time. Penny would remember. She did remember my parents, and that my dad was into music. She paused and nodded.

"You look just like him," she said with a smile.

She knew right where her old directories were and promised to head straight home after church to find them.

It wasn't long before she called me back with addresses on Lacomb Drive and Providence Road. Those names jogged my memory and I knew I was on the right track. They both had nicknames in our family, "The Swamp" and "Windy Hill". I didn't know what it would be like to drive to the old places, but it didn't take nearly as long as I figured.

Both properties had current residents, were locked and gated, and had no trespassing signs. Neither had the mobile home we had lived in on it anymore. Seeing the place was cool, but it didn't seem worth it to disturb a family to look around at buildings we hadn't lived in. I had the rest of the day free, so I decided to do the other walk my mom said I should do.

My dad's family moved back and forth between Bisbee, Arizona and Oregon several times. When they were first in Oregon my dad was pretty young. The family lived in a boxcar, as my grandpa worked as a welder on the Southern Pacific railroad tracks. When they moved back my dad was a sophomore in high school.

This time they lived in a house they purchased in Sodaville, which at the time was a decent sized little town. My dad now owned his Model A but it remained in Bisbee at the homestead. He walked from Sodaville to Lebanon where he went to school on a regular basis. The walk, assuming he went into south Lebanon, would have taken him somewhere around an hour and a half to two hours. This was the other walk I planned to do.

I drove the back way from our old place on "Windy Hill", to Sodaville and parked at City Hall. City Hall is about the size of a coffee shop, a large shed or small workshop. It was the only place I knew I could park without being on someone's property. City Hall was Sodavillle's downtown.

The view re-entering Sodaville, OR

I spotted a community board with the town's history posted for visitors to read. It once boasted motels and tourism due to what they believed were medicinal soda water springs. Seemingly just before my dad's family moved there the government condemned the spring due to contamination. I suppose the cost of living had gone down a bit after that.

The community board also warned of a recent large cougar sighting in town. Being mauled is low on my list of desired experiences, but I really wanted to do this walk. I reasoned that there were probably more cougars in these parts when my dad lived here and he survived.

I "Googled" how to survive a cougar attack. "Speak with authority and fight," was the answer. I practiced in my mind. "Come on...I'm going home to my family whether you like it or not!" I'd say authoritatively. Meanwhile I'd be grabbing stones and sticks. Finally, I'd yell like Thor going into battle and charge the beast. I had a plan. Time to walk.

I wasn't wearing sandals this time, but I did have a couple-hour walk ahead of me. I had to go mostly downhill toward south Lebanon and then turn around and do the same thing uphill to get back to the car. I judged that I had plenty of daylight. I had a half bottle of water. I had legs with at least twenty percent of their energy left. I had a pair of canvas skate shoes holding my raw and itching feet together.

As I walked back and uphill from Lebanon, I was really beginning to feel it but I'd just encourage myself to get to the next landmark and methodically stride ahead. If I found beautiful things to look at as I walked, it took my mind off the disintegrating feeling between my toes.

"I'm almost to that turn at the stop sign...OK...I can see the farm with the llamas and one's out front to have his picture taken...then there's the house with all the cool Volkswagen trucks and old Fords in the driveway...then the old baseball field...then the row of old houses where Dad might have lived." After that row of street side houses there was one more fairly steep hill remaining and I was back to modern conveniences. One step at a time. I made it back without incident.

There's something I've noticed can happen when you do something like taking a long silent walk. Neither of these walks included headphones or phone calls. I noticed you might start off with some stuff on your mind. You begin to mull that over as you walk until it finally resolves or sort of floats away for a while. You may pick the train of thought back up. You may not. You may just begin to get enthralled in the view.

Much of this is because you won't be getting anything done anytime soon. You won't be getting anywhere quickly. You won't be implementing any solutions to your problem right now. You won't be catching a quick glance at the scenery while you're off to the next thing. Rather, you'll be enjoying the scenery as you slowly study it from different angles.

There really is an element of endurance to it all. There's the physical endurance to be sure. I apparently need to work on that part. But there's also a mental endurance you cultivate on long silent walks and the like. You will be processing your inner life, your goals, and your ideas very slowly and from every angle. This I am often too busy to experience if I'm honest.

My dad loved to walk. He didn't mind driving either, but walking seemed to be some sort of escape for him. Or was it a discipline? Maybe it was a little bit of both. My aunt tells me he loved to get out and run through the trees in Oregon as a young guy. A neighbor girl used to join him, she told me, and people thought it was a bit odd. They thought maybe they got off in the woods and did something wrong. They weren't doing that at all; they just discovered a common passion best shared. The girl went on to be a track athlete in college. People, I guess, just couldn't understand why two young people might want to be traveling on their feet when they could be transporting themselves with a machine like everyone else.

You do get some weird looks when you're walking. I think people assume you're up to something or trying to scout out and steal their cars...I mean...why else would you not be driving? As an older man in Tucson, my dad was known for walking around. He was the white-bearded man in a plaid or flannel shirt just strolling the neighborhood. Friends have told me that they saw him regularly on their commute.

My parents moved a few houses down from my family a couple years before Dad died. They weren't big fans of the city, but they came to be close to us. And now Dad walked the city neighborhood streets. One time a neighbor, who had apparently seen him walk by a number of times, came out and told him in all seriousness that he was "keeping an eye on him". My dad just said, "OK" and didn't walk down his street anymore. Little did the guy know that my dad lived a few blocks away in a decent home with three vehicles in the driveway. I bet he would have been happy to know such a guy was "keeping an eye" on the neighborhood for us all from ground level if he had looked into it. Instead he assumed he was some kind of vagrant.

As I walked between Sodaville and Lebanon, I became acutely aware that that I was getting a lot of sideways glances. The worst was one I walked right into. I spotted a yard full of cool vehicles including four modern Volkswagen quad-cab trucks and a couple of classic Ford trucks...one the same style and color scheme as my dad's F-250.

An older teenage guy was in the yard and I called out to him to ask where you get a VW like that and what year the Ford was. He seemed very uncomfortable and gave me very vague answers. Then his mother came hastily outside with a worried look on her face. I explained to them that I was taking a walk to Lebanon and just noticed their cool vehicles.

The looks on their faces told me that this information was not making me look any better in their eyes. I excused myself without further conversation and thanked them for taking the time to talk. They didn't answer me back. A couple of times on my walk a cool Volkswagen quad-cab truck passed by me with the father and mother of the family in the cab. I'd like to think they weren't keeping an eye on the strange walking guy, but who knows.

At one point a guy in an old Toyota pickup slowed down and yelled out to me, "Need a ride into town?" I yelled back that I was enjoying the walk, and he looked slightly confused. He slowly sped up and moved along...his cigarette smoke trailing like a ribbon from his window. I felt a little better knowing that someone was at least comfortable enough to be around me.

I approached one other person, and that was only because my half bottle of water was empty. A guy was unloading his minivan in his front yard, so I asked if he had a water spigot available to refill my bottle. He looked at me with nervous eyes, but then seemed to make an inner decision.

"I got a new water bottle for you." he said.

"Oh, that'd be great!" I sighed as I replied.

He left for a moment, came back with the water bottle and handed it to me with a smile.

"Thanks! My name's Andy." I smiled back.

"Have a good day Andy." He turned and walked back to his car.

I guess a walking guy was still too risky of a guy to entrust his name to, but that's OK.

My dad liked to walk because he had discovered the joy of it in his childhood. In his adulthood, though, he read Peter Jenkins' Walk Across America and decided he wanted to walk even more. He started to view walking as a better way to learn about places and a way to observe and deepen your understanding of people.

Peter Jenkins had been pretty disillusioned about his country, but he reported that his walks had helped him connect more with it and see that there was far more to the people he encountered than he had seen in the newspaper and on the evening news. It seemed to give him a lot more perspective about the tumultuous times he was living through as a young man.

I wonder how many complexities of life my dad mulled over, then set aside, and then returned to contemplating later as he walked. I wonder how many of those peaceful spaces of time helped him to put up with his limit-pushing, big-idea-developing, over-opinionated, and typically ignorant son. However his walks figured into all of that, they were at least the embodiment of one of my dad's most respectable characteristics: his patience.

His patience was evidenced in many ways, but something I realized looking back is that there were so many ways in which my mom and I lived that he wished were different. He knew we should spend less money. He knew we should think more before we spoke.

I'm sure he had a lot of thoughts, but he never seemed in a particular rush to fix anything. He would mention something from time to time, perhaps share a principle he believed to be true, and then he'd just let us have space to mull it over and let discovery take its course.

At some point my choice of music and entertainment went from mild and fairly innocent to vulgar and obscene. It all started when I heard some west coast gangster rap in middle school, loved it, and started looking for more music like it.

One time at a sports card shop, I bought a couple CDs I'd never heard of from the display case. To this day, I don't think I've heard anything as obscene as those two albums, but the content at that time intrigued me. It was like forbidden fruit. I wanted more.

I began buying more of the music and posters of the artists. Some of it I decided I could show my parents, but a lot of it I tried to keep under wraps. I'd listen to it only on my Discman in the secrecy of my bedroom.

I can guarantee that my parents were concerned with the type of content I was pumping into my mind. My mom was more vocal about it, but I know it concerned my dad as well. He wanted me to grow up to be the kind of man that would be a blessing to his family and community. He didn't set out to raise a violent man who mistreated women and smoked copious weed. Men often go the way of their heroes, and my heroes were quickly becoming exactly the type of men my dad didn't want me to be.

One day my dad and I took a fairly long walk to a local buy, sell, and trade bookstore in Tucson. Knowing me, I spent the time talking his ear off about all the things I was interested in at the time.

When we got there, I spotted a movie on the shelves that I'd seen before with a friend. It was something of a spoof on other movies about the inner city and ghetto culture. It was vulgar and obscene to say the least. Women were objectified and demeaned, racial groups were mocked, and violence was treated like a sideshow joke.

I asked my dad if he would buy the movie for me. He took a long look at the back of the jacket and finally...hesitantly... said, "Oh...I guess so". I couldn't believe it! I'd snuck an awesome movie right under his nose. He had no idea what he was buying for me!

On the long walk home he was pretty quiet, which wasn't too surprising. My mind was racing. I now had access to this movie whenever I pleased...at least, that is, on my VCR in my bedroom on LOW volume or when my parents weren't home.

As we walked into the house we saw that my mom still wasn't home. My dad casually sat down and kicked back his La-Z-Boy recliner and said, "Hey son, I think we'd better watch that movie together." My head spun. I tried to explain that it probably wasn't really his style of movie. He casually said, "That's ok Andy, let's go ahead and watch it while your mother's out."

I reluctantly inserted the tape into the VCR. It was one of the most uncomfortable hour-and-a-half spans of my life. My dad watched it all...and I continually glanced back at his face. When I'd laugh at a scene or a joke, I'd look at him. He wasn't laughing. He just looked a little heartbroken. When the movie was over, he simply looked over at me and said, "I think we'd better return this, don't you?" And by that time I couldn't have agreed with him more.

We took the long walk back to the bookstore and back a

second time that day. This time on the walk back, though I was tiring, I also felt as if a weight had been lifted off my shoulders. Dad never explained exactly why he'd suggested taking the movie back. In fact, he never brought it up again.

He didn't need to bring it up again. Just being in his presence watching that movie had been so uncomfortable. And it had exposed me as the perverted kid I had become. I didn't want that discontinuity in my life. I didn't want to do things that couldn't be done in his presence...things that broke his heart.

My dad could have said "no" at the store, but my desire to watch the movie would have just been fueled by the prohibition. He could have criticized my taste in music and clothing at any point, but that would have just driven us apart. I wonder how much he thought that through as we walked silently down the road together on our way back home from the bookstore. However much he considered it, he came up with the perfect plan.

My dad's patience with me as well as his willingness to play the long game, even if he left a lot of smaller battles uncontested, paid off. I valued his love and our relationship so much that I wanted to please him. When my shame was exposed in his presence, I didn't want to run away from him, but from the things that didn't measure up to his character. And I was so happy to be back at rest in my relationship with him...even if my legs were tired.

7
Honesty

"A man's character is like his house. If he tears boards off his house
and burns them to keep himself warm and comfortable, his house
soon becomes a ruin. If he tells lies to be able to do the things he
shouldn't do, but wants to, his character will soon become a ruin"
Ralph Moody - Little Britches

On the way to one of the pre-Oregon day trips I took to
Bisbee, I stopped by my dad's grave in the Veterans
Memorial Cemetery in Sierra Vista. The gravestone was
finally set and the flood of emotion that came while I was
reading the simple headstone caught me off guard. I sat
down on the freshly laid piece of sod that covered the pine
box casket I'd made for my dad's body just the week prior.

His was the second casket I had made in the wood shop.
It was simple and unassuming, yet sturdy and made with
care. It reflected well on my dad. My dad didn't leave much
behind, but all who knew him mourned his passing. In him,
we lost someone we could trust and depend on. In retrospect
I appreciate him more and more.

Each time I visit the gravesite, I'm torn considering how
long to stay. Nothing could be more obvious to me than the
fact that he is not there. That was obvious to me the moment
he died. His body lay there, but my dad did not. I felt no
impulse to talk to his body. At the same time, though, there
is a certain comfort to being spatially closer to the body that

once held your beloved.

I sat on the grass for a while thanking God for a dad I could miss and mourn. I let my thoughts wander to the good times, and all the ways in which I appreciated him. It dawned on me that this commemorative stone felt appropriate in his case. There are no gravestones in eternity for the saints. But this would be his stone of remembrance until the day death is undone.

A few miles down the back road between Sierra Vista and Bisbee there lays a derelict ministry campus that stands out dramatically against the dry desert landscape. Its sanctuary is massive, with a prominent cross-capped dome over the vestibule. The property is expansive, boasting residential and educational buildings and a once fully functioning airstrip from which the pastor and his traveling team would arrive to and depart from revivals they would host throughout the country.

From a distance it's very impressive. Up close you're struck by the decay. The roof wore down years ago, and the sun now shines through the weathered boards. Most of the windows are broken out. Everything is in disrepair. Once vibrant paint is now faded. Windblown debris has collected in every corner.

The pastor, A.A. Allen, is buried and memorialized on the property. Allen was one of the early televangelists and had been given this land just south of Sierra Vista back in the late 50's by a loyal follower. He had broken off from a Pentecostal ministry that hadn't validated his claim to have a call from God to preach after the discovery of some issues in his life. He pressed forward alone and figured out how to broadcast his healing crusades, in which he would pause mid-healing to advertise his books in front of a nationwide audience.

He made quite a name for himself and still has a following to this day. Even my non-church-going grandparents listened to him on the radio according to my mom. His messages would bring my grandma to tears. His ministry center is now under new ownership. A small group of hopeful folks there are waiting for the revival of the "revivals" that once happened there on a weekly basis. Allen is credited with not only building the church and ministry center but also the town itself. The town is named after the commodity that became his claim to fame: Miracle Valley.

The remains of A.A. Allen's ministry center in Miracle Valley

The trouble with remembering A.A. Allen, though, is that he was a two-faced man. Some try to overlook it, but others can't see past it. He would strongly condemn the "demons" of his time, be it lust, alcohol, witchcraft, disease, or denominations like the one that rejected him, while he remained enslaved to his demons behind the scenes.

A few reports came in that he seemed intoxicated after crusades. These allegations were not new: the Pentecostals knew he had been arrested for drunk driving in his early ministry days. He vehemently denied it all, and his close associates covered for him. He claimed that Satan was just trying to destroy God's work.

When his wife left him, the facts behind their troubles were not released to the public. His personal life was kept carefully under the cover of his security detail and a strict policy of non-disclosure. Nobody could cover the scene in his hotel, though, the day he died. Bottles and pills littered the floor. He lay slumped over a table, wearing only his underwear, his urine pooled underneath him. Evidence of a life destroyed by hiding the truth. His last big feature in the media was the exposure of his shame. The coroner's report found he had died of acute alcoholism and, therefore, liver failure.

Who knows how much of that ministry itself was fiction over fact, but we do know that his life came to a very sad end. The great edifice he built now stands as if a monument to shattered aspiration amidst the arid grasslands of Miracle Valley. One has to wonder if it could have been different if that ministry had been one in which telling each other the truth was more important than keeping up appearances.

Allen was a pioneer of racial integration, boldly opening his doors to all peoples. He was gifted to say the least. I am sure that his words encouraged many people to change their lives for the better. His words may have influenced my own family toward a life of faith in God and away from besetting sins. But, unfortunately, his great ministry center now reflects the condition of his character. His character had become a ruin, and soon after his "house" followed suit. It could have been different.

Not long after my dad died I started reading Ralph Moody's Little Britches, a book my dad had liked when he was a young man. I began to see why he liked it. It gave him a window into a father-son relationship he had never experienced. Charles Moody taught his young son to guard his character, and Ralph's mother instilled in him the words of Scripture.

"Measure twice and saw once," was Charles Moody's advice to his son as they worked on their house together. That was a line I recognized from my dad. He made sure to teach me that specifically, among other things. He was taking notes from Charles Moody, a man he wanted to emulate, for the day when he would be a father.

I can't recall a time I ever felt deceived by my dad, and he always encouraged me to tell the truth. Later in life I was deeply wounded by the lies of others, and the pain of betrayal was hard to bear. My father, though, provided an environment of truth, though he never bragged about it. He taught no class and spent little time condemning the lies of others, but he personally resolved to be a man of character. I knew that I could always fall back on him when others I had chosen to trust with my heart had ripped the foundations of trust out from under me.

I once had to fire a thief from a Christian bookstore that I managed. It was such a painful experience! It was so sad to investigate the problem, state the evidence, and then to be accused of injustice by this employee that I deeply desired to trust. It was so hard to discern the truth that lay underneath a facade of righteousness. It was a truth that, as a young man, I truly wished I hadn't had to see.

I was also conned by a man claiming to be a fellow Christian. He used the church as an in-road to trick an idealistic young man into giving him money. Looking back, I never felt comfortable with the guy, but I wanted to believe that everyone who claimed to follow Jesus was actually trying to do so. He got four hundred dollars out of me before I finally was able to accept that I was being lied to. These aren't even the worst lies I've been hurt by. Oh how I wish the list wasn't so long!

It truly saddens me to think that some people, when they reflect on the lies told to them, immediately think of their fathers. I have the gift of being able to look at my dad as a contrast to the lying lips of those who hurt me.

Later in his life my dad worked in an alloy shop that made metal machine parts and wire. These parts were critical to production of their final products. They made some of the elements out of platinum. The platinum was so valuable that the employees weren't allowed to talk about it with outsiders. No one could leave the facility until they accounted for every bit. They had to weigh the precious metal in and out. It seemed, though, that someone found a loophole. If the platinum went out with the garbage it could go un-detected. The thief could nonchalantly excavate it from the dumpster after work.

My dad had been somewhat demoted. At his age, the company knew he wouldn't be with them too long. He wanted to work day shifts instead of nights, but those shifts went to the younger guys the company wanted to retain. A supervisor informed my dad that he probably would never get off of nightshifts in the role they hired him for, but that he could work days as a janitor.

My dad had invested money and time in courses at the community college to get a more respectable job. He had worked so hard on nightshifts, hoping for a promotion. He had achieved employee-of-the-month several times. The last thing he wanted was to downgrade to being a janitor. But he also wanted to have more time with his family and night shifts were making that goal unattainable. He took the lower position though he felt it was unfair. Why couldn't they pay him what he deserved and move him to the better shift after years of serving the company?

All that could have made him bitter. It could have pushed him over the edge. It could have led him to seek out a way to get what he deserved through less legitimate means, but he didn't succumb to those temptations.

One day, as my dad performed his newly assigned janitorial duties of cleaning the toilets and taking out the trash, he spotted a bar of platinum in the outside dumpster. He would never declare that he knew for sure, but we assume that it wasn't delivered there by accident. Who accidentally tosses out a weighty bar of precious metal with the paper towels and candy wrappers?

A dilemma now stood before him. If he returned it, he might risk the anger of a thief. He also had an opportunity to keep the valuable bar of metal for himself. Our family sure could have used some extra money. He could have capitalized on the opportunity since he didn't even have to sneak the metal out of the shop himself. Somebody had done the hard work for him. Instead, though, he quietly turned in the valuable bar of precious metal to his supervisors without assigning any blame. He did what was best for the company. He did unto them, what he wished they would do for him.

Few people knew my dad returned the platinum as the employees weren't even supposed to talk about it. My mom and I know because we wondered why he brought home the $25 gift card to Applebee's and an "Eagle Eye" certificate they awarded him for his honesty. He never retold the story that I'm aware of. But I, his son, will never forget it.

I am tempted to lie, cheat, and steal on a regular basis. I want to be a man of character like my dad. I pray I have the grace and resolve to be honest like him, especially since I have the gift of him teaching me how it's done. Many of us haven't had a dad that exemplified honesty, or any number of other characteristics for that matter. I hope you see in my dad's story that you can choose to go a different way yourself. My dad learned the way of honesty from Ralph Moody's father on the pages of a book. We can do the same; no matter how little experience we have with it in person.

Sometimes, of course, the truth can really hurt. And in many cases honesty isn't restricted to the simple choice between lying and stating the facts about a situation. Often honesty is the careful telling of truths that carry great relational importance and have the potential to do real harm if wielded incorrectly.

My dad was a fairly honest man but he, too, had to accept the honesty of others; one of the most difficult situations of all to face. Telling my dad the truth proved to be one of the most difficult things I'd ever have to do. The little man motif suited my dad well, and in many ways he exemplified the good within it.

As with all of us, though, a dark side lurked underneath the surface. For my dad that dark side included the blaming-of-others, self-pity, and self-deprecation. He would self-deprecate to the point of shirking personal responsibility for his failures. Throughout my life I felt sorry for him. I always wanted to help him and come to his aid. The truth is that he should have stood against his fears and come to my aid far more often than he did.

I have become very comfortable on the counselor's couch. Several rounds of trouble in life pushed me there. The first round included my dream job falling apart and a miscarriage. I struggled to wrap my mind and heart around those losses. They were soon eclipsed. My best friend and his fiancé were about to get married. I was to be the best man. On the way to Tucson they lost control and rolled their vehicle. Both of them died; she on the scene, he at the hospital. We had a double funeral on their wedding day. Then...not long after...my first marriage ended in a chaotic whirlwind of discovered lies and affairs and threats of self-harm. My daughter was hardly one year old.

I had never thought of going to counseling before that terrible couple of years. All of a sudden, I couldn't seem to get by without it. I lived for the next session. At the beginning I was sure we would rehash my recent tragedies over and over until I felt better. When my counselors went after my relationship with my dad it threw me for a loop. I couldn't believe it when they suggested that he had failed to love me in many important ways.

I resisted the diagnosis. Then I thought back about the times I got mad at him. I thought about the times I'd lashed out at him. The time I called him stupid, yelling at him until he got angry and in my face.

Why was it that I looked back at his reaction and was grateful for it? It's because I'd never seen him fight for himself and, in so doing, for me. He'd been the king of rolling over. He'd been a mule, carrying the burdens of others with head down and worse...complaining about it. He left my mom's emotional care to me because it overwhelmed him. He left me to figure out my future, giving me only the advice of not being like him. He'd really let me down.

The counselor asked about baseball. I loved baseball but a crummy coach had spoiled the sport for me. I knew I was good. I had a killer fastball. The year I moved up to juniors, the coach played his son at pitcher and not me. In fact, I played about an inning a game. None of it made sense to me, but I concluded that I must not have had what it took in his mind.

The next year I played again, but halfheartedly. The year after that I just quit. One of my high school English teachers encouraged us to write a paper about our biggest disappointment in life and mine was easy. "Yield of Dreams" I called it, lashing out at the coach who picked his son over me even though his son wasn't all that good.

The only redeeming moment of that story was me making the final play of the season, in which we won the championship. Coach had shoved me out in left field for my one inning in the bottom of the ninth. The game was close and the other team's power hitter was up to bat with two outs. I filled the least important space on the field, but the towering fly ball came to me and not his stupid son. Vindication! No, it really wasn't. I'd still warmed the bench almost all year, and anyone can catch a fly ball.

"Why'd the coach sit you out?" the counselor inquired.

"Oh, well, I found out later!"

When I'd written the paper for English class, my mom proofread it. One day on the way to school she asked if I wanted to know why I didn't play.

"Uh, yeah...what do you mean?"

My coach owned a local sporting goods store. We had the

coolest uniforms in the league that year; pinstriped pants and fitted caps...home and away uniforms. My mom proceeded to tell me the rest of the story.

The coach told the parents about his plan to have the best-dressed team in the league. The team would have two uniforms instead of the one league provided team shirt. Of course his store would be ordering the uniforms. It would only cost an extra hundred bucks or so payable to him. My parents couldn't afford the upgrade. Coach's plan to get his money was benching me until they paid for it. The league required coaches to play every kid at least an inning a game. My parents refused to pay more than the families assigned to other teams, and they didn't have the money to spare. I warmed the bench, completely unaware of the underlying drama the whole season.

"What a jerk, huh! Can you believe that?" I looked at the counselor.

"Where was your father?"

"Huh?"

"Where was your father? If that happened to my son I would have told him he'd better prepare for a fight. I'd have reported him to the league. I'd have put you on another team so he'd have to face your fastball and his choices."

It had never crossed my mind. He could have done something, but looking back, he was invisible...cowering under the shame of being poor. He'd let me down. I'd never seen it. It wasn't the only time.

The day I told my dad the truth, about how he'd hurt me, is burned into my mind. I didn't want to hurt him back. I wanted to run. I had to look him in the eye and articulate that his neglect had placed all sorts of burdens on me that no child should have to bear. No child should have to help hold his mother together on her bad days. No child should be left sitting on the bench suffering an unjust punishment for being poor. No child should be sent into the world with the mission of "Don't be like me." I told him I believed in him too much to accept what he'd given me as good enough. He could have done better.

"I love you Dad, and that's why you need to know that I KNOW you could have done better, and you can, starting now."

"I know...and I'm sorry," he replied sincerely.

That wasn't the only time we had that sort of conversation. Once on a walk he complained that he'd never had enough money to buy a house, and I had to disagree.

"You did, Dad, you guys just spent it on other things. You knew we wasted money a lot, but you didn't stop it."

"I guess so..." he mumbled.

"I'm not mad at you, Dad. I just can't let you shift the blame every time."

Another time it was a complaint about not having money like other people and, thereby, not being able to do fun stuff. The lack of contentment was sickening. He'd been able to travel, fix up his Model A, and own an Airstream for his train sets and, on top of that, his family loved him.

"Dad, I'm sorry. Not that you don't have what other people have, but that you're so miserable and discontent... that's just sad."

This clearly frustrated him. His temper flared more than I'd ever seen.

"Dad, listen to yourself! Why are you so angry?"

"I AM NOT angry"

"Oh yes you are! You need to face this, man. It's eating you alive."

These conversations were never easy. In fact, they were downright torturous. The last thing I'd ever wanted was conflict with my dad and, even worse...to hurt him. I knew his story and wanted nothing to do with driving the knife of insult deeper into his chest. On the other hand though, to wallow in self-pity was to reinforce the lies that told him he was a nobody. I can honestly say that my hope was to instill that he was able to stand and be a man. That he wasn't too stupid or slow. That he could be "the little man," and hold his head high and take responsibility.

I didn't fix him. I did, though, experience a deeper relationship with him. To his credit, he would receive every hard word given without holding it against me once he had the chance to stomach it. Not once did I sense that he was begrudging the day after. You can tell the difference between the wounds of a friend and the wounds of an enemy. Honesty inflicts only wounds of love and is pained that they are painful. That I learned, not from, but alongside my dad.

8

Simple Things

"Want to take a walk?"
Leroy Littleton

The coffee shop in Old Bisbee had grown too loud. The seat felt increasingly uncomfortable. My mind wandered from weariness. Much of the day lay behind me. I had to make a change.

My go-to activity these days is to take a walk. You never know what will come of a good walk. It's far different, you see, than taking a drive. On a drive you see the beautiful countryside flying by, but you don't see the distinct blooms on the bush that protrudes out across the sidewalk. On a drive you see the breathtaking panorama lying out ahead. On a walk you see the panorama too, but you also sense every nuance of the earth beneath your feet. On a drive you get to your destination, while on a walk you may discover a destination you couldn't have planned for if you tried.

I packed up my writing gear, laptop and notebook and stashed it in my truck. I grabbed a flannel shirt and set out for who-knows-where. My dad had taught me what to do. You just walk. When you're done, you're done. You don't need a specific place to go, but you can head toward something.

Why not? If you really want to enjoy yourself, take a camera and snap photos of interesting things. My dad's camera was typically attached to the third button of his flannel shirt and tucked in the left side pocket. That way it was easily accessible while protected from slipping out in the event that you bent down to pick up something interesting you'd found.

I set out from Old Bisbee southeast. All the other neighboring towns lay ahead. I considered walking to Warren, where the wealthier of the mine's employees once lived and the old baseball field stood at the lower end of a beautiful city park. Downtown Lowell, always photogenic, was on the way too, and a small community called Jiggerville used to exist out there somewhere.

All of it lay past the Lavender pit, a massive open pit mine that stopped production in the mid-seventies, though I could swear we would see trucks driving up out of it when I was a kid. I've driven around the Lavender pit many times, but can't recall if I ever actually walked around the whole thing. What strikes you first, when walking, is how massive it is. The majority of the town of Lowell was displaced to dig the pit, and that becomes more and more believable as you pace the edge. Halfway around, it appears as if it could swallow the town of Bisbee whole and as if Bisbee is hiding back in the canyon west of the pit for dear life.

The Lavender Pit from the viewing area

You notice, too, the fact that the sidewalk is permanently stained by the runoff from the dark orange copper-stained rock walls that project up from the pit's edges. You notice where a car once crashed through the steel fence posts and wonder if it fell down into the pit.

A viewing area is situated about halfway around where tourists can stop for photographs. A building is there, boarded up these days. It used to be a store full of Bisbee Blue turquoise, unique to the Lavender Pit, and copper jewelry. I remember my dad saying it was too expensive for him. Many things were too expensive for our family back then.

Amidst the viewing area stands a massive stone monument to Harrison M. Lavender, the guy whose idea the pit had been, and who had led Phelps Dodge to make it happen. I read it all for the first time before I walked by. As I continued around the pit, it dawned on me that none of the thousands of men who labored in the pit got a mention. I'm glad Mr. Lavender got a monument, but I don't suppose he would have gotten too far without his crew.

Once I had successfully made it around the huge pit, I was near old downtown Lowell. The downtown strip is all that's left. The majority of the storefronts are dusty with neglect though staged as if in business. A popular restaurant called Bisbee Breakfast Club has transformed a couple of them and kept the traffic flowing through the area. The old theater is now a contractor's shop. A motorcycle mechanic has set up in one of the old garages. A collector, or group of collectors, has positioned their cool old cars along the curbside. Lowell appears frozen in time when Bisbee Breakfast is closed, as it was when I walked by.

I passed under an ornate old underpass that ducked beneath what used to be a railroad. I then walked back toward the old Lowell School where my dad started first grade in 1950 and attended as an eighth grader in 1957. The school is still active, and an older brother parked to pick up his younger brother late. A graveyard stood to the north, and I wondered how many of the bodies lying in there belonged to the workers who dug out the pit. How many of them were here when Bisbee was compared to San Francisco. What would they think about the state of the town today?

I started to realize that walking the neighborhood that lay ahead wasn't what I wanted to do. I was starting to get some of the awkward looks you get when you walk places. A lady was coming out to her car and seemed very nervous to see me walking by. A man exited the neighborhood church, put his head down, and got in his truck without looking me in the eye. He drove the same kind of Toyota truck that I had parked back in Old Bisbee. Assuming he was the pastor, we had the same profession. The difference between us was that I was on foot.

I turned around just after the church and headed back. The school seemed empty now. The streets of Lowell were less busy. The motorcycle shop's door had been bolted closed. The contractor's truck sat offloaded and done for the day. The sun was beginning to duck behind the mountains and a slight chill became evident in the air. It had all been fairly uneventful, but a nice break.

As I neared the end of downtown Lowell, though, I noticed that something was going on that interested me. An old Ford box truck had been sitting out near the edge of the Lavender pit for years. It had a mural on its side advertising the town of Lowell. I saw it was now turned backward. A large cloud of blue smoke was bellowing out from an old GMC Suburban with engine revving behind it.

As I walked closer I realized that some guys were trying to tow the old truck up the hill backwards, but had just run it up against a curb and blown one of the dry rotted old tires. I almost walked by, but instead I yelled out to one of them asking if they needed a hand. He beckoned me over to help push the huge truck back and off the curb.

We failed at the push but eventually the old Suburban was able to pull it down and off. The next step was getting back to pulling it up the hill. The old Suburban looked to me like it needed a tow itself. The hood was partially propped open, and the paint was faded in a "been sittin' in the backyard" sort of way. It bellowed out the blue smoke of burnt oil every time its owner revved it up, but it had four-wheel drive and an old V8 engine that could. The men realigned the old box truck's front wheels. One of the guys volunteered that the truck was a 47 Ford that used to be a bread truck over in Willcox before it was re-purposed as a school bus. Now it lived on as a billboard for Lowell. The guy behind the wheel was the owner. He was a little peeved that he now had to find a tire to fit his old twenty-inch rim.

The owner of the Suburban locked the hubs. I took my newly designated position atop the hill communicating the status of the box truck to the guy in the Suburban. We all gave the thumbs up, and he slowly crept the old trucks up the hill. At one point I saw the box truck was headed toward the curb again. I'd like to believe I saved them from certain disaster. Once up the hill the four of us gathered for a bit to review our work. I thanked them for letting me be a part of the action and they thanked me for my help.

As I walked away I heard one of them comment to the other that I seemed like a nice guy. It brought a smile to my face. The feeling of mental fatigue was gone. I felt invigorated and full of life. I was excited to walk back around the Lavender pit, even though the sun was behind the mountains and the chill was becoming more acute. Good thing I had a flannel under my arm!

The box truck adventure begins

I often don't get around to taking the long walks my dad was known for, but I can't remember one I regret. Almost every time I take one, I find my mind has cleared at the end of it, or I end up with a good story to tell. Sometimes the result is a great idea or a sense of resolution on a matter that's been bothering me. Other times I just take note of interesting things I would have driven by and missed every other day in the hustle and bustle. And on a really great day I find the walk has slowed me down enough to meet someone new or experience something interesting.

Just days before I'd been walking my own neighborhood, which I had to actively decide to do instead of watching TV, and I met the guy down the street who also had an old F-250 in his yard. It turned out it belonged to his dad before him and he had decided to hold onto it. We swapped a couple of stories before I shook his hand and offered that I hoped I'd be seeing him around. He seemed like he hoped for the same. The simple thing...the little decision to get outside and take a walk...had another wonderful and surprising result.

My dad didn't do a lot of big things and he seemed not to mind the fact a bit. In one sense he saw big things, as beyond his reach but in another sense, they weren't even his style. The bigger the event, the more hoopla, the less he seemed drawn to it. He never suggested throwing a party or making a big to-do about anything that I can remember. If there was any draw to something big for him, it was that he could blend in behind it and do his own thing.

Dad was more the type to enjoy the simple things. He drew fulfillment from some of the most basic of pleasures and these sustained him throughout his lifetime. The most noticeable of his pleasures was that of simply being outside in the fresh air talking a walk. He was prolific on his feet. His workout gear was a pair of plain black non-slip shoes he also wore to work, a pair of jeans in his early years...pleated black pants in his latter, and his signature long-sleeved plaid or flannel shirts. He didn't walk to be in shape, though he saw the exercise value. He walked simply because he loved to take a walk.

On his walks he also found a number of other simple things to enjoy. Most notably, he loved to walk with someone, though he wouldn't go out of his way to say so and few people would offer. When he was younger he had his running mate in the forests of Oregon. When he grew older he had me when I wasn't too caught up with the busyness of my life.

He knew that I liked to go get coffee, so he'd offer to buy me a cup if I'd make the coffee shop a destination to walk to with him. We'd try to take some form of back way, using side streets and cutting through the backsides of shopping complexes. The back way was less disrupted and offered other perks.

Quite often my dad came home from a walk with a full pocket or with something in his hand. He was always on the lookout for little treasures. On a rare occasion he would find a big treasure that he'd have to cruise his truck back to pick up.

The little treasures were typically pieces of metal and, for years, every aluminum can he saw. He would crush them and carry them with him the entire way. These he gathered because they were his ticket to getting other things. He would collect, and Mom would sort, metal objects into his little hardware organizer back home, depending on their usefulness. Many times we found just the thing we needed in that little organizer amidst some home improvement project or repair. Usually they were items he had once picked up on a walk.

He also picked up every single coin he saw. He was never one to neglect a quarter, dime or nickel, and especially not a penny. Not only did he pick up every penny he saw, but he did so with a certain enthusiasm. He was on the search at all times for wheat pennies. I'm not sure when he developed the love of monetary medallions, but I know that he kept interesting coins from at least as far back as his time in the military.

His goal was to have one of every year of wheat penny, but he had no problem with having more than one of each. When the Treasury released quarters representing each of the United States, he became much more enthused about quarters, too. If the coin he found wasn't special, that wasn't a problem. It could still go in his coin bank to be cashed-in some day for a surprise amount of spending money, or he could use it to trade for a special penny.

To him, the "Give a Penny, Take a Penny" tray at a store or restaurant was an opportunity for him to trade up. He would examine every coin in the tray and, if one were somehow special, he'd casually swap it for one in his pocket that was more run-of-the-mill. Though I can't claim to have adopted his passion, I also find myself picking up every coin I see lying on the ground. I also do at least check to see if it has some special characteristic.

Perhaps his favorite thing to look for on walks corresponded with his favorite type of walk to take. Having grown up on the railroad, he loved to walk down railroad tracks. I think he liked that they were a little less busy, but also that he could frequently come home with some railroad spikes. When I was growing up, there was always a little pile of railroad spikes under our porch that he'd brought home from a recent walk.

He saved the spikes for some sort of potential project. One time he gave a box of them to a friend who welded them up into the shape of a windmill at his request. His old house in Bisbee had a windmill and having a throwback to it made of railroad spikes brought a smile to his face. It sits in my back yard these days.

I've taken a couple of railroad walks recently and each time with my dad in mind. The first was in Albany while awaiting a chance to talk to the mechanic at the exhaust shop. I can't recall if I arrived before he opened or when he was out for some reason but, whatever the case, I found myself with time on my hands. The exhaust shop was next to a convergence of railroad tracks, and there was no question where I wanted to walk.

The second railroad walk was on my last getaway to Bisbee. Down near the border there is an old railroad track that once served the mines. The lava-rock bed and small trestles are still there, creating a natural path through the desert.

On each of my railroad walks, I too returned with a handful of metal. In Albany the railroads were active, and spikes were plentiful. I snagged one to make sure I had a real Oregon spike to keep in the truck. It's living on in the F-250 these days. I'm saving it, of course, for some kind of project someday. Maybe it will become the shift knob, or get welded onto the truck for some kind of function. I grabbed the spike that was in the best condition. Perhaps it had never actually been driven into the tie.

As I walked down the track by the border near Bisbee, I realized that I was not the first to go spike hunting on this trail. The track had been removed over ten years prior and there's no doubt the area was regularly scoured. In fact, I'd later have a conversation with a couple of guys who walked it regularly and always kept an eye out for old metal objects as well as the copper ore that had fallen from old freight cars back in the day.

I walked for some time and there was nothing to be seen. I kind of had my hopes up that I would come back with a little memento by which to remember my dad. When my dad would walk, he'd be very attentive to his surroundings. Sometimes he would wander off to investigate something I'd have never noticed.

On this particular walk, I passed over a small trestle and noticed that the ground was still soft from the rains a week before. It also appeared that the earth had been slowly eroding down off the trestle on each side. There were a number of scraggly bushes that looked pretty well established down below, and it crossed my mind that maybe some items would have washed down and become lodged near the base of these bushes in years past. Perhaps the new rains would have uncovered something.

I walked down near the bushes to check on my hunch. It wasn't long before I stepped on a metal plate of some kind. Then I saw another like it with what looked like a spike head on top of it. I kicked at it a couple of times and, as the earth dislodged, so did nine rust-encrusted railroad spikes. As I picked them out of the dirt I could tell they were older. The sizes weren't uniform, but close. I gathered them up excitedly and hauled them back to my truck.

It's strange to describe the joy that I found in discovering those spikes. Sure, it was because it was something my dad and I would have enjoyed together, but I also think I experienced a bit of the excitement he would have enjoyed if it had just been his little adventure.

The spikes instigated a flurry of questions. How old were they? Were these forged by hand and would that account for the lack of uniformity? When was this railroad built? What was it for and where did it lead? It was an enjoyable train of thought to consider.

The next day at the local farmers market a guy was selling some railroad spikes and I was able to strike up a conversation with him about the ones I found and the railroad. The simple act of finding an interesting thing gave my mind a welcome break and served as a connecting point with another person. Such a simple thing had become a profound gift.

The cans my dad would crush and pick up on his walks all came home too. He would load them into a wheelbarrow that he kept covered over by the shed he and a friend had built. About once a month he would have his can day on which he'd bag all the cans and take a relaxing trip over to the scrap metal recycler. He would stand in line to have them weighed, and then he'd get in another line to pick up his check.

Back when he lived in Oregon he got into the habit of collecting cans because they got you ten cents for each. Arizona didn't reward the recycling of a can nearly as well though. I know because I once took a whole truck load of metal to the scrap yard and walked away with twenty-some bucks. His cans were "clean", but I still can't imagine he made enough money to make his trip technically worth it.

Perhaps I just misspoke. To him, the process was worth it…though it wouldn't be deemed worth it to many of us. But consider his can gathering from another perspective. Litter is a problem and it clutters up our neighborhoods. Bluegrass music is beautiful and makes people smile. My dad turned trash into bluegrass. Clutter transformed into a smile.

My dad, in the collecting of his cans, was able to give himself a goal that fueled being a good neighbor. He picked up the cans that somebody was going to have to pick up. Then he took a little trip to the recycling place that "wasn't so bad really." On the way back he passed by the used book and music store where that cash was often traded for bluegrass albums. His collection of them grew steadily over the years. He had a tote bag he kept in his truck full of them.

I remember one year my dad asked for "one of them nice stereo systems" in his truck for Christmas. At that time he had a little 91 Ford Ranger that I'd originally bought, but didn't like. I was working in car audio at the time, so I snagged the truck and didn't just put in a new radio. No, I went all out. He got a CD deck, speakers all around, and an amp and subwoofer behind the seat.

He loved it, and every time I'd borrow the truck one of the bluegrass albums was on. The sub brought out the bass tones you usually didn't hear. Of course, this was not what any of our other customers at the stereo shop were listening to, but it made my dad smile. Picking up trash on the roadside fueled that smile. It was definitely a worthwhile use of time.

As I headed back to Bisbee to write and remember, I knew what I wanted to play on the stereo as I drove. I didn't do CDs anymore. All I had to do was type "bluegrass" into my phone and there they were...any album my dad could have ever dreamt of. The music has a certain levity that I'm not accustomed to in most of the music I grew up on. Some of the songs are playful in nature, while others utilize a catchy tune and a story to say pretty meaningful things.

I was hungry as I drove but was waiting to catch one of the little breakfast spots for a meal before I went on with my day. Another thing that always seemed to bring my parents joy was a good breakfast out.

When we first landed in Tucson we were really low on money. That remained the case for some time. When we moved out of the Shady Haven Mobile Home Park to a little better spot up north, we were close to the railroad. I bet the rent was low partly because the train went by and blew its whistle throughout the night. This, of course, didn't bother my dad a bit and we all came to sleep better because of it.

There was a seedy bar called Generations a few miles from our house that served an "early bird" breakfast to entice the morning crowd. If I remember right, the bar was also open pretty early. It also happened to be near the tracks. Our family's little Saturday treat became a long walk down the tracks or a short drive over to "the greasy spoon", as we called it, for a breakfast out. The food was OK, and if we all got "the special" we could live it up without breaking the budget.

As the years went on, "the greasy spoon" closed down and we weren't quite so broke. My parents came to love going out for breakfast as their little treat. When I grew up, that would be the regular event they'd invite me to. When my daughter was growing up, the restaurant that moved in a block or two from "the greasy spoon," had a sweet potato pancake that she loved more than anything. It came to be known to the waitresses as an "Abby cake." Abby would recognize the intersection near the cafe and sing out "Pancake!"

Abby would always ask "Papa" to have an "Abby cake" with her. It became their sweet but simple tradition for years of her life. My dad always gave the waitresses a "hard time" about something and, of course, on the way out he would sift through the "Give a Penny Take a Penny" tray for wheat pennies.

As I arrived back in Bisbee I pulled up to the local breakfast spot, not the biggest and most popular one, but the one that was a little off the beaten path and full of locals. I got some coffee and asked the waitress what was good. As I sat there sipping on my coffee, it dawned on me that life doesn't get much better than eating delicious food that someone who loves to cook is serving you as they make a living for them self.

Sometimes I still get the special when I go out, and sometimes I splurge for the omelet like I did in this case, but I hope I never forget what an absolute joy it is to get to go out to breakfast. Some people, like my family for many years, consider it a rare treat. So I gave the waitress a hard time and enjoyed every bite. They didn't have a "Give a Penny, Take a Penny" tray, but I'll keep my eye out.

9
Faith

"I don't know."
Leroy Littleton

When back in Bisbee for the second time, I went to church in the small town of Naco twice in one day. Naco is right on the U.S.-Mexico border and a mere fifteen minutes or so south of Bisbee. My friend Jesse is the pastor of one of two stateside churches there. His church also hosts a service in a church member's house across the border in Naco, Sonora.

When I first met Jesse, his role as a pastor in the small town intrigued me because my dad's cousin used to host family reunions there. I wanted to hear more about his work, which led to us becoming friends. Most Arizonans have never heard of Naco, so having Naco "in common" is a pretty special thing.

At that one family reunion I remember, we gathered at a hotel right next to the Port of Entry. I ran around with some of the other kids and we wandered across the border and got shooed back across by the man on watch. My only other memory is that of being downwind from a foul-smelling cigar that gave me a stomachache. Apparently, the cigar belonged to the unofficial "mayor of Naco," my dad's cousin. Thanks to his mayoral influence that day, I never desired to smoke anything ever again.

Naco, the town, is very small, especially in the States where it's technically labeled an unincorporated place. By nature of being in a small "place", a community the size of a typical rural high school, Jesse's churches are small, too. Jesse serves not only as the pastor, but also as the song leader. He commented that his percussionist likely wouldn't be at church to accompany him that Sunday.

When it comes to music, percussion is about all I can boast (and I'd be a fool to boast about it), but it is something I used to do to help out at church. I hadn't played in church in eight years or so, and it kind of sounded like fun, so I offered to step in. Jesse kindly accepted the invitation of a guy he'd never heard play before. I played at the stateside church in the morning but there were several kids at the church in Sonora that liked to jump on the drum. I happily stepped aside so they could jam that afternoon.

As we set up for the stateside service, Jesse entered lyrics into a computer to project onto a screen so people could sing along. He hummed the tunes of the songs as he entered the lyrics, and a memory flashed into my mind. Jesse was humming a tune I knew... *What a Friend We Have in Jesus.*

The tune immediately transported me to my childhood. I thought of my dad pulling out his old Martin acoustic and finger picking the same tune. It was one of his go-to's. Before my lifetime especially, my dad played in the Lebanon church band on a regular basis. He also played in a local band that toured around the area to play at churches, events, and for charity. He wasn't one to lead with his words, but he loved to serve the church using the talent that he had...and his talent was playing guitar or bass in the back of the band.

I hadn't foreseen that jumping in on percussion would remind me of my dad but it brought up more than a memory. I realized in that moment that he had instilled my lifelong bent to serve God and to get involved in the church. To this day serving the church is something I love to do.

I didn't play flawlessly that morning. An eight-year break had left me a little rusty, but I tried to put my soul into the rhythm as I sat behind Jesse and the other singer. Most of the songs we sang were newer, ones my dad had never known, but then we sang *What a Friend We Have in Jesus*. The small congregation raised their voices together in simple faith:

> *What a friend we have in Jesus, all our sins and griefs to bear;*
> *What a privilege to carry everything to God in prayer.*
> *Oh, what peace we often forfeit, oh, what needless pain we bear,*
> *All because we do not carry everything to God in prayer.*

Naco Christian Church in Arizona (Top) and Sonora (bottom)

An incredible thing can happen in a community of faith, committed to a standard outside of itself and to one another. Such a community can bring diverse people together while both affirming and correcting them in love. Jesse was amidst leading the people of his church through the book of Exodus (not the easiest piece of ancient literature to trudge through). Though his church met at two different times and in two different countries, Jesse sought to maintain unity between them. They prayed for one another, shared their resources with one another, and listened to the same words from the same Scriptures each week.

The week I came to town proved to be a particularly unique time in Naco. The midterm election had just occurred in the States and border issues were a major talking point. Bisbee had been abuzz with political conversation; especially since an Arizona senate seat was still too close to call. In Old Bisbee folks gathered in the coffee shops bemoaning the President and hoping things would turn the direction of tolerance and acceptance. In the surrounding rural areas, folks who felt that law and order were in jeopardy praised the administration and hoped that someone would finally get tough and get some things straightened out. This was a divided community.

On top of all that, the town of Naco was on a rare state of alert. In the news they'd heard that the US military was being sent to the border in their backyards. Thus far they hadn't seen much, but all of a sudden that weekend Humvees full of soldiers had driven into town and parked along the border fence near the Port of Entry. Mexico's army was present on the other side of the border as well, in greater number than folks were used to.

The media was closely following a migrant caravan coming up from South America, since the President had declared his concern about it. Folks on both sides of the border were unsure how to feel about it. Some Americans feared the type of people that might be in the caravan and the trouble they could bring if allowed into the States. Others asserted that we had all once been migrants and that our values of human rights had to upheld in offering asylum.

In Mexico some folks worried about what would happen if the caravan ended up stuck at the border and they had to absorb the thousands of strangers in their midst. Others related to the migrants and hoped they would be able to come and find safe passage.

Jesse's Scripture text that Sunday had come from his natural progression through the book of Exodus. He taught his folks on both sides of the border Exodus 22:16-27. The text included what Jesse's Bible titled as "sundry laws". It began with a law prohibiting seduction of a woman by any man not her husband. This law could apply to Jesse's communities and in the broader national conversation. The #MeToo movement was big news and people were trying to define the sin of sexual harassment and how to enforce laws to curb it.

The text went on to prohibit sorcery, bestiality, and sacrifices to false gods. The people didn't seem too alarmed by these prohibitions. They all seemed to assume that such things were off limits.

The final law had to do with exacting unfair or ungracious interest upon those in need of a loan. This bore more application in this impoverished community. Many had been victims of some form of predatory lending or had struggled to be generous to those they doubted they could trust.

The laws in the middle of the text, though, required the most comment. Exodus 22:21-24 felt particularly pertinent. Jesse preached through it carefully, but with conviction, on both sides of the border.

"You shall not *wrong a stranger* or oppress him, for you were strangers in the land of Egypt. You shall not afflict any widow or orphan. If you afflict him at all, and if he does cry out to Me, *I will surely hear his cry*; and My anger will be kindled, and I will kill you with the sword, and your wives shall become widows and your children fatherless." - Exodus 22:21-24 ESV (emphasis added)

Of course, Jesse had before him folks whom this text impacted in numerous ways. His church, being south of Bisbee, he had some of the rural folks who tended to the right of the political spectrum. He also, though, had folks who had come to Naco from Old Bisbee. The methods and opinions of the current administration didn't fit the Old Bisbee mindset well at all. He had folks who were recent immigrants. He had longtime Arizonans who felt that they were unfairly treated at the Port of Entry because of how they looked, regardless of their legal status. They could name specific agents who made their skin crawl.

In Mexico a small crowd of orphans, who would take the bus to the church every week, sat under his teaching. Widows gathered on both sides of the border with varying experiences of and leading to their widowhood. He also had, as does any room with people in it, folks who were guilty of, or complicit in the guilt of, breaking these laws God had given in the Bible. The victims were also perpetrators. The lines between the two were impossible to draw.

Jesse applied the Scripture to all who sat under him with loving care. He declared innocence for no one. He condemned no one. No one stood beyond redemption. He offered hope to all. By faith in a sacrificial Savior, who bore upon himself the curses of breaking God's law, they could have a second chance to sing "What a friend we have in Jesus". Humbled people could be free of their "sundry sins" to live a life that was honoring to God and loving to others again. He encouraged all to consider what God's words might mean for them. They could strive for law and order and have deep compassion for the strangers among them. With the guidance of God over all, they could move through their differences together.

Jesse's humble leadership, and his churches' collective submission to the same God, made this possible. A diverse group of people continued to gather together in unity, though an iron fence and military vehicles stood between them.

My dad was always inclined to foster relationships with people different than him. I would credit his time in the mills, his churches, and his time in the military with teaching him to do this. He had friends on all sides of the political debates, and they felt comfortable talking to him. He had friends of all races, first evidenced by the photos of him and his closest friends in the military.

Dad and a close friend of his in U.S. Army

When he worked in the lumberyard and the alloy shop in Tucson, he always got along with African American, Asian and Hispanic guys he worked with. In fact, some of them were his biggest fans.

I'm not sure what exactly he heard from his pastors over the years, but he sure was committed to reading his Bible. I assume he had read Exodus 22 dozens, if not hundreds, of times throughout his life. Through his example I learned to steer clear of polarizing politics because it didn't build relationships. His consistent church attendance and Bible reading taught me to look outside of myself, or popular opinion, for the truths that can critique and affirm us all with equal force.

In my mid-twenties I got a job working with students at a large church in the affluent foothills of Tucson, and Mom and Dad decided to visit. New visitors were always followed up with a phone call and a visit from a few of the sweet, dedicated folks of the church.

I wonder what the team was thinking as they drove toward our family's mobile home on Star Grass Drive, a pitted dirt road lined with dusty mobile homes...mostly old...some with barking pit bulls behind the chain link...one with a toilet serving as a front yard flower pot. Of course, at the end of the road they found a sweet older couple whose mobile home was quaint, but meticulously maintained.

The feedback from the visitors was that my parents were very nice, but they weren't sure if my dad had ever become a Christian. I can imagine the scene. My mom gave very articulate answers, expressing a few points of dissent from the visitors' point of view but, by and large, coming across as quite full of faith and the knowledge thereof. My dad, on the other hand, probably answered, "I don't know" to a number of their questions. I imagine this because he answered, "I don't know" to the majority of my questions. There were a few things he felt a lot of clarity about. His boss got paid disproportionately to the amount of work he did. Eating right was THE key to long life and good health. Eating out was a waste of money. I've concluded he may have been wrong about at least two of those. You decide which two.

For most of the big questions, though, Dad gave you some form of "I don't know" as an answer. I'd ask "What should I say to the girl I like?" The look in his eyes and the words of his mouth were in perfect harmony, "I don't know." He didn't know. He'd never been a wordsmith to say the least. My mom initiated their relationship, at least verbally. He kept visiting her bookstore. He claimed no ulterior motive, but my mom thought otherwise. Mom says that he chased her till she caught him. Mom struck up the conversation. They were seriously dating in no time. So, no, he didn't know what to say to a girl.

The same was true of his interactions with God. What the visitors didn't see, as they didn't know him, was his regular (never advertised) reading of the Scriptures and a whole host of books about being a disciple of Jesus. He chased God.

They didn't see him choose to love deeply, even when he'd been shown little of what love looked like.

They didn't see him choose joy in the face of all the evidence that life was full of sorrow.

They weren't there when an angry driver gave him the finger and yelled at him because our old Ford Pinto burned oil. Dad waved kindly at him and looked over at his young son in the passenger seat and cracked a smile... "Hey, maybe that guy wants to help re-build the ole' engine. Should we ask him?" I never forgot that moment.

The visitors never saw how peaceful he was amidst a frantic world. While all my friends' parents were rushing around building their lives, my dad would carve out hours to walk the railroad tracks to pick up cans and railroad spikes. He got his bluegrass CD money with those cans. A lot of that music was full of lyrics about Jesus and what he had done on the cross. He soaked up the good news as he drove back and forth to and from work.

The visitors never saw how incredibly patient he was (most of the time) with a wife and son who could really test his limits. They never saw how incredibly kind he was to everyone he met, especially those "down on their luck." They never realized how well he lived his life...deeply committed to the moral structure in the Scriptures that he'd hidden in his heart over the course of many years.

They never saw how faithfully he offered his love and life to others. He was the only sibling in his family who ended up getting married once and staying married for life. He worked faithfully for his employers even when he felt it wasn't fair.

They never experienced his gentleness. He was the gentlest man I could imagine. And they never saw how he controlled his actions in order to honor God and others. He refused to speak ill of my mother, even on the days she betrayed all her articulate words.

Love, joy, peace, patience, kindness, goodness, faithfulness, gentleness, self-control; these are the Apostle Paul's evidences that someone is united in faith to Jesus by God's Spirit..."the fruit of the Spirit," the final fruit being a confession that Jesus Christ is Lord and that He came in the flesh.

My dad's life bore much of this good fruit. So much that his "tree" stands out in the orchard of humanity as I've experienced it. Few would know that better than I.

But what I also know is that if you asked my dad what he'd say to God if He asked him why He should let him into his heaven...that he would say "I don't know." Why? Because he didn't. He didn't presume to know what he'd say in any situation. He refused to act sure when he wasn't. I know that many of us who profess faith do quite the opposite. We articulate statements of surety that betray our doubts. I know so because I do that sometimes.

On my final hike with my dad, in the Chiricahua Mountains, I had resolved to learn more about him. One of the things I most wanted to know was more about his faith. I had a number of questions ready for him, and most of them didn't get us too far. He had a lot of thoughts about certain portions of Scripture, especially ones that had to do with health or with the book of Revelation but even then he expressed a lot of ambiguity about the exact meaning of it all.

At one point I asked him if he ever had any doubts. As he slowly made his way up the trail in front of me he sighed...

"You know, we all have our doubts...but sometimes you experience things that make you believe."

"What would be an example of that?" I inquired.

He simply replied..."Oh, days like today."

A day with his son amidst the beauty of creation. That's all it took to remind my dad that he really did have a Father in heaven that it all pointed to.

I'm so grateful that my dad shared his simple faith with me. I'm glad I got to catch him reading the Bible on a regular basis. I'm beyond grateful for the simple applications he shared. He always prayed a short and simple prayer before our meals together. Once I criticized him for saying the same thing every time. He looked over at me gently but firm...

"I suppose I could go on and on like a hypocrite."

He caught me off guard in the best way. It dawned on me that he knew the words of Jesus and actually sought to apply them. His simple faith, rather than being an attempt to do the minimum, worked itself out carefully. Jesus had hard words for some people who came across very religious...who had almost all the right answers. My dad's faith stood not on his performance or what he knew. It was founded on the Savior who did know the answers, and His words.

When my dad stood before God after he breathed his last here on earth, I believe that Jesus spoke up for him. Who knows what He said...maybe "I love Leroy, and Leroy listened to me." Or maybe He said, "Leroy chased me till I caught him."

10

Gentleness

"Gentle Husband
Dad & Papa"
Leroy S. Littleton Jr.'s Epitaph
Veteran's Memorial Cemetary - Sirra Vista, AZ

My earliest memory of my dad, perhaps my earliest memory of all, is of him crouched down on the kitchen floor of our mobile home on Lacomb Drive with me. We were rolling little handmade wooden cars he'd made back and forth to each other across the yellowed linoleum floor as I smiled with joy. These were the types of memories I hoped to add context to as I drove out to our properties near Lebanon where I lived as a child.

Other memories included washing the cars with my dad in the front yard with our shirts off, spraying each other with the hose. Blackberry bushes grew all along the roadside. I remembered picking blackberries with Mom and Dad on the front of our property, and eating most of them before we got back inside.

The most vivid memory was of Joe the goat escaping the pasture behind our home and banging his horns against the front door. My mom opened the door and tried to move him away by grabbing his horns. He didn't budge. Sometime later he meandered out to the road and stood in the middle of it. I recall being quite transfixed by the whole event. Then I saw my dad's F-250 coming down the road toward Joe. Dad jumped out to save the day. He wrangled the beast back through the gate into the pasture on our little hilltop property.

I parked a little bit down the street from each of our old places and took walks by them so I didn't come off as too creepy. The first place, on Lacomb Drive was the most interesting.

It wasn't completely fenced off like our other place. I wanted to walk all around the property but figured I'd better stick to street side. I began to wander into the trees around the perimeter at one point and stepped on a small snake. I'm sure the little guy was harmless but I was sufficiently deterred.

As I stood back looking at the old land we once called home, I couldn't help but realize that I'd had a sweet childhood. My memories were all good from these places, and I truly wished I could come up with more of them. My parents had to work a lot more than they wished they had, but I have no recollection of that. I remember being a happy kid with room to run and play. I remember being so excited when my daddy would come home to play with me.

The week after my dad died, our family had to figure out all the things you have to figure in the wake of a loved one's death. It was difficult to do. Where would he be buried and in what? How much were we going to spend on it all? What would he have told us to do if we'd had more time to plan for this? Should we buy a headstone?

We opted for the Veterans Cemetery that stood between Tucson and Bisbee. Mom liked it and I drove by it every time I went to Bisbee for a day away. That settled the headstone discussion too. The Veterans Cemetery provided them so cost wasn't an issue.

Then we had to choose twenty-some characters with which to describe him on his headstone. That proved to be one of the easiest things to figure out. One word resonated with us all. Gentle. He was a very gentle man. Including that sufficiently satisfied us all.

My dad was employed in the type of industries where you worked long hours and those hours were very taxing on the body. I remember him coming home with the look of exhaustion on his face. I don't know why, but these facts didn't deter me at all as a kid.

"Daddy, come play with me!"

"Daddy, let's go run around the house!"

He would sigh a deep sigh... sometimes utter a slight argument for doing something more low key, but then would invariably give in and run around after his energetic kid. Later in life, he'd come out and play baseball or basketball until sundown or suppertime.

Earlier in life he would just walk around with me on his shoulder. Though I don't remember it, he and I apparently had a bit of a routine when I was little. I'd hold a plastic milk jug in my hand, and he'd pick me up and put my head on his shoulder. He would walk me all through the house and get me nice and relaxed. He couldn't see my eyes, but when I dropped the jug to the floor, he and my mom knew I was officially "out" and they would tuck me into bed.

Dad putting me to sleep with the milk jug

We have a photo or two of him carrying me on his shoulder and I looked so at peace in his arms.

This side of him didn't stand out to me as much in adulthood until my daughter was born. My dad was the sweetest grandpa you could imagine. I learned he'd always wanted me to call him "Papa" but, for some reason, it never stuck with me. I called him "Dada," "Daz," and then just "Daddy" or "Dad."

My daughter Abby, though, from the very start, called him "Papa," and was clearly drawn to him. He'd hold her on his lap with Christie, our miniature dachshund. He read her stories. And he would carry her around on his shoulder until she fell asleep. He got to know her until her last year of elementary school, and her natural impulse was always to crawl up on his lap or ask him to pick her up. They had a very sweet relationship.

We have an old photo of him carrying me on his shoulder as a baby. One of the photos we took of him carrying his granddaughter turned out to be almost identical. He wore a plaid pattern shirt and had a little blond baby perched on his shoulder; one of his arms supporting underneath; his other hand gently placed on the baby's back. We have the two photos framed together, a lasting tribute to the loving care of a gentle soul. Both his son and granddaughter were at perfect peace in his arms.

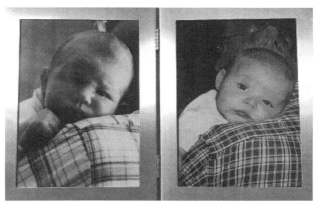

Baby Andy on "Daddy's" shoulder and baby Abby on "Papa's" shoulder

At his memorial service, we put together photos for different parts of his life and accompanied the short slide shows with older country music he liked. We had trouble fitting all the photos of him and Abby behind the Judds' song "Grandpa." When it played, Abby cried as she buried herself in my wife's arms. This part of his life few people got to see. We had a good number of photos of him playing with Abby, but so many of him carrying her in his arms. Several of his friends commented that he talked about Abby all the time.

My second trip to Bisbee was almost a year after Dad died. I wanted to reflect some more. I wanted some more time to feel the loss of him. Jesse, the pastor in Naco, graciously offered his guest room free of charge for three weeks. I'd never been to Jesse's house but was grateful to have a spot to make a home base. He asked if I was cool with there being a dog in the house. Not only was I cool with it...this made the arrangement so much better in my mind.

Fiona met me at the door the night I arrived at Jesse's house. Fiona was a cute old mutt and I immediately dropped to the floor to greet her and scratch her behind the ears. I knew I'd love having Fiona around.

Jessica, Jesse's wife, warned me that Fiona usually would bark at a guest every time they left the restroom. "She'll think you're coming in for the first time every time," she told me.

I laughed and told her it was no problem. My dog Benji back home could be pretty on edge. He and I get along famously, but some other people just worry him...especially people he isn't as used to. In fact, whenever my dad would come over he'd growl and bite him on the shoes. After he got that out of his system he would curl up next to my dad on the couch. Jessica assured me that Fiona might be like that, but not to worry.

The next morning when I awoke, I shuffled into the restroom to shower up. On my way out I assumed I'd get barked at but, instead, Fiona was curled up in front of the bathroom door wagging her tail. When I fully opened the door, she sat up and tilted her head toward me. I bent down and scratched behind her ears.

"Oh, hey there. Fiona...I guess I'm not so bad, huh..."

She let herself into my room behind me to hang out. Every day from then on I had a rug of a dog lying somewhere close by whenever I was at their house. Fiona was my new buddy.

I'd like to say I was always that good with animals, but the truth is that I wasn't at all. Christie, the dachshund I had growing up, was my Christmas present when I was about twelve years old. To be fair, I'd asked for a golden retriever type dog for Christmas. I was very hopeful that some full-size dog would be awaiting me on Christmas morning. Christie fit nicely into my stocking. I didn't have a big stocking... and the stocking had other stuff in it too. She was a baby miniature dachshund. My parents had picked her out because we all liked a dachshund our friends in Denver owned named Torquey.

I thought Torquey was cute, but not what I had in mind as my dog. Baby and miniature were

Christy was not the dog I had in mind.

not adjectives I had in mind for my personal boyhood dog. I wanted to have a dog I could play catch with. If I threw a ball at Christie, I'd probably kill her. I wanted a dog that would defend me when I took it with me to the park to play ball. Instead, I could carry little Christie around in my baseball glove. I guess it was kind of cute, but also very disappointing.

As the years went on, I'd kind of roughhouse with Christie for a minute or so, but then I'd move on. Dad would tell me I was being too rough with her and that she wouldn't like me unless I treated her nice. I didn't think he knew what he was talking about. I'd rile her up to get her to do something interesting. She'd play along for a bit but then move on from me. I'd feel sort of rejected and annoyed.

As time went on, I began to notice that she didn't seem too interested in me, but she became like my dad's shadow. All he had to do was plop down on his La-Z-Boy and say, "Come here, Tisty." She'd hop up on his lap and he'd gently scratch her behind the ears and pat her a little. Then he'd leave her alone. She'd nestle in between his leg and the arm of the chair and get comfortable. Every once in a while he'd give her another little pat or a scratch. She was his buddy. Her whole life, it was clear that she loved being as close to my dad as possible.

My dad always had a way with animals. The Bisbee homestead featured a herd of dogs when I was a kid. Grandpa took in any stray that wandered onto the property. As you drove down the rutted dirt driveway the dogs would meet you and surround the car as you approached the house. My favorite was a little black and white mutt named Seiko (say-ko), who was a little bigger than the others and had more energy. Seiko was a mutt, no golden retriever, but still the kind of dog I wanted some day. The kind you could really play with as an energetic boy.

There was one dog my dad and I were both a bit unsure of. It was huge. To me it was the size of a cow...some sort of Great Dane-Brontosaurus. It was a bit much. When you parked the car, there it stood inches from the window. You had to look up to see it's massive mouth gaping open and full of teeth to greet you. Risking your life you opened the door. Standing to your feet, you braced for death. He would sniff you, and move on...to kill another day.

I don't know when my dad first connected with animals, but I wonder if he learned something back as a young man. We have some photos of a dog that seemed to belong to his family during his childhood. He kept those photos. His dad didn't treat him with gentleness, but he somehow learned that when he was gentle and kind to an animal, it would stay true to him and become his close companion. He tried to teach that to me, but I was slow to learn.

Eventually, about the time I was ready to move out after high school, I learned to be gentle with Christie. She started to choose to sit with me a little more. One time I remember her burrowing herself in my pillow before I went to sleep, and I woke up with her snoozing under my neck inside the pillowcase the next morning. I loved it.

These days I own two little dogs...zero golden retrievers. Of course, I can't rough house with them too much, just like Christie. One of them, Benji, is my special buddy. And I love just scratching him behind the ears and having him curl up on my lap. He burrows under the blankets next to me every night. He was clearly abused before my brother-in-law found him on the street in the middle of a summer rainstorm. He was scared of everyone and defensive. With time our family won him over. I knew what to do because my dad had taught me to be gentle. I just wish I'd learned the lesson earlier.

Dad of course, didn't limit what he learned about gentleness to animals. He applied it across the board. He was gentle with his wife. He was gentle with his son. He was gentle with his granddaughter. And we all felt a deep attachment to him because of it. We all loved to be in his presence. So upon one of the veteran's gravestones in the Memorial Cemetery in Sierra Vista, AZ are the words, "Gentle Husband, Dad & Papa." They suit his memory well.

Dad's headstone at Veterans Memorial Cemetery in Sierra Vista, AZ

II

Encouragement

"I'm proud of you, son."
Leroy Littleton

My confidence level hit rock bottom as I approached Bisbee for my last round of writing. I wasn't sure if writing about my dad was of interest to anyone but me. I had planned to drive the F-250 this time, but one of the rear brakes was sticking and the power-steering hose blew the day before I planned to hit the road.

Before leaving I sent out the chapters I had written to some trusted friends for review. A subtle terror was sinking in as I imagined their critiques. I listened to some writing podcasts on the road, which wouldn't have been an option in the old Ford, and I became overwhelmed by the amount of focused work it would take to write a book well. I have a pretty full life, and I knew I couldn't focus on the project like some of these writers were doing.

I arrived at Jesse's house in Naco as a podcast ended. I wavered between keeping my whole project private, or sharing it for anyone to see. That evening at the dinner table Jesse asked how the book was coming along. He too had lost a father and had a particular interest in my journey. His dad died of Lou Gehrig's disease when he was young.

Jesse listened to me as I told him about my trip down from Tucson, the podcasts, my concerns, and the hopes I had for the next few weeks in Bisbee. He didn't approach me as an expert, but he assured me that my time was being well spent.

"I'd read a book like this!" he exclaimed.

Jesse went on to discuss other similar stories that he had heard about and wanted to read. He reminded me that my dad and folks like him were worth listening to, but so easily missed in the midst of all the loud voices dominating the bookshelves and airwaves. He told me that he knew specific people whom he thought would really like a copy of a story like this. I really needed my friend's encouragement that day. My resolve returned.

My dad was not a man of many words. He would tell me he loved me, but only from time to time. He didn't give a lot of specific directives for me to follow. He didn't assume upon me all of the plans he had for my life. As far as I know, he didn't actually have any specific plans for my life or for his own. I was never aware of any sort of "game plan" or strategy we were employing for success. Despite all that wasn't there, I would still describe my dad as very encouraging.

Looking back, it seems to me that he was most interested in discovering me as opposed to defining me. I wonder if he remembered his passion for music and creativity and wished his father had been more interested in discovering those things rather than trying to get him to go out shooting to become a man. Many of my life's pursuits were foreign to my dad, but he encouraged me to do them anyway. Whether in sports, being a leader, or recording a podcast...he learned to support me in pursuits he didn't understand. His support was subtle but stable.

One thing I wish my dad would have understood more was how much I wanted to be like him. I think he believed that lie that he was a nobody...that he was too stupid and slow to be a role model. He had no idea that in my mind he knew everything about building stuff. It didn't register with him that I wanted a car because he talked to me about his old cars, and I thought the kind of old cars he'd had were amazing.

He didn't understand that I thought he had a cool job at the lumberyard, especially when he drove the delivery truck around town piled high with building materials. He drove a big flatbed truck and got to see all the construction sites. He always seemed to know where things were being built.

The one time I got to ride along was one of my greatest childhood thrills. At that time his company hadn't bought the trucks with hydraulic dump beds yet. Dad would un-strap the big load of lumber, throw the truck in reverse, back up fast and slam on the brakes. The bunk of lumber would fly off the flatbed and skid across the hard desert ground. Then he'd get out, cut off the bands with the contractor and jump back behind the wheel of the big truck. He got to where he knew his way all over the city without a map. I thought my dad's job was cool...and that my dad was cool.

When I got older I couldn't understand why my dad began to talk about my future in terms of not being "like him." He wanted to see me go to college so I could get what he would call a "real job." I reacted by doing the exact opposite. The week after high school graduation I jumped into working with my hands.

Car audio was my only idea. I got into it in high school with a few of my friends. My sophomore year I paid $75 to get a stereo I found for sale in the newspaper professionally installed. That felt like a ton of money to me, so I went home and uninstalled it so I could see how it was done. From there I started telling friends that I could install their stereos for $25 a pop. I usually did it right.

Dad liked cars. I liked cars. Dad worked in a shop. I would work in a shop. So the week I graduated I walked into the premier car audio shop in Tucson and asked for a job. They started me at the bottom, but I was fine with it. In my mind I was asserting somehow that my dad's way of life, having sought out a job right out of high school, wasn't something to be ashamed of. I remember telling him that there was nothing wrong with being like him.

Of course, my dad had other motives I didn't understand behind his advice. He knew that jobs in the trades and service industries were hard and that, in his experience, the only ones who made any money were the bosses and the owner.

In the stereo shops I learned that a lot of guys felt that way. I remember the ways they would talk about the owner of one shop. They saw him as unwilling to get his hands dirty but getting most of the profit. I remember one of the best workers quitting one day and starting his own business because he thought the pay wasn't fair. In retrospect I can see that my dad was trying to save me from that struggle.

These days I can see even more angles, as I've had the opportunity to be not only a laborer, but also a manager and a small company owner. I can't say I've figured it all out. Being an owner and boss is way harder than my dad or I ever realized. The burden of responsibility is a unique workload that taxes the body by way of the mind. Taking care of employees can be very hard, especially when profit margins are small. I often reflect and wonder if I'm doing an OK job of it all.

One thing that I feel deep inside, though, is a conviction sown within me by my dad. In a sense, I've still rejected his goal of me not being "like him." On the other hand, I am humbled that I am in the place of "owner" or "boss." Though I often fall short, I have a deep desire to see the employees I oversee taken care of. At the least, I want to make sure that I am not profiting at their expense. His indirect encouragement to me has been to make sure that in my work, the people employed by me get paid first and get paid fair. Also, I came away encouraged to be willing to jump in and get my hands dirty myself and to find ways to serve others.

In his final years, when he was retired and in his seventies, I had the chance to hire my dad to help with a few projects. He assisted my buddy Sean and me on a job site or two and in our custom shop. He was slowing down and didn't have the strength he used to, but his work ethic was impressive. I hope he could tell how much I appreciated him. I hope I'm becoming the kind of business owner that he could have respected.

*Dad helping Sean mix concrete in the old Midtown
Artisans shop*

My dad's primary form of encouragement, since words weren't his thing, was to get involved and help out. When I bought my first house, my dad would come over any time he could. He wasn't always the expert on the project, but he would quietly jump in and help in whatever way he could.

The same was true when my wife and I bought a home that wasn't move-in ready. For a month he'd come after work and help me out, often until dark.

He was also generous with his time serving those in need. One time a group from our church was helping a guy purchase and move into an old mobile home that had been pretty trashed. The whole job was less than glorious. We were peeling rotten paneling off the walls, raking piles of trash out of the yard, and scraping gunk out of every crevice. The jobs everyone wanted were the ones that left you with the greatest sense of accomplishment, like tearing off the sagging deck or putting down the new flooring.

A woman from our church had graciously taken on the cleaning of the bathroom and had found it difficult to penetrate the layers of grime. Unbeknownst to me, my dad had peeked in and had asked if she needed any help. She later told me that he decided to focus on the toilet and that he quietly got to work as she took a break. When she came back, the toilet bowl was shining. My dad had not only cleaned it, but had done an incredible job.

For the last couple years of my dad's life, my parents lived down the street from my family and me. He'd take his usual walks and would always pass by our place. Often I wouldn't be home, but if I were he would check in to see what I was up to. If I were working on some kind of project, he'd always stick around and help. I came to assume that he'd always be by my side whenever I had a project.

My church started looking into leasing or buying a new meeting space. I offered that I could help fix up whatever we found. I knew my shop could be of use, but I also told the rest of the team that my dad could come over and help me out most days. I didn't even ask him beforehand because I knew he would always be willing. That's just the way he was. If there was a need, and he was free, he was willing...especially if I was there.

I had some really exciting news. I had stumbled on a cool old building that looked abandoned. Weeds were rampant on the lot, but it was in a great location for our church and was the perfect size. I reached out to a contact listed online, and heard back. It was looking like the owner, the president of a historic men's club that had not actually abandoned the building, was willing to sell it to us for a price we might be able to handle. I wasn't sure about the situation yet, so I hadn't even shared it with my parents.

Before we could have that conversation my mom called to tell me that Dad's recent digestion issues were getting worse and that she was taking him to urgent care. He had tried a weird cleanse involving some clay, which made me roll my eyes. I assumed his "health-nut" tendencies had gotten him in trouble. I talked to him and flippantly chided, "Dad, you ate CLAY...What were you expecting?"

The urgent care, though, sent him to the hospital where they scheduled an emergency surgery to clear the blockage. Forty-five minutes later we learned he had pervasive cancer. The surgeon told us he might only have days to live. "Maybe months," he added "...but maybe just a few days."

All of a sudden my building project, which was SO exciting to me, became a lower priority. I hadn't seen this coming. My dad had been over to the house just a little while back and had helped me hang my gutters on the back porch. He had seemed a little more tired than he usual, but then again...he was seventy-three years old. He was still taking his walks. We had walked down to the neighborhood bookstore not long ago. I could have sworn I'd seen him walking the street just days ago. I was not ready for cancer. Neither was he.

I decided that I would go to the hospital as often as I could and have every conversation I could possibly come up with. During one such conversation, he asked what I was up to other than "this." I think he was a little tired of talking about cancer, and death, and cancer, and cancer, and cancer. I told him I had found a building for the church and asked if he wanted to see pictures. He did, of course, and I told him all about it. Then I asked him, "Dad, what do YOU think about this? Is this a good move? Am I getting us in over our heads?"

"Andy, you get that building and move your church into there!"

He had never given any of my ideas such an emphatic affirmation in my life.

"Really, Dad?"

"Oh yeah, I doubt you're gonna find a better one than that."

The photo I showed dad of the Knights of Pythias building we ended up buying for our church

Boy did I need that encouragement, both then and in the months to come. Buying that building and moving into it would prove to be a layer of one of the most taxing periods of my life thus far.

We had to fundraise, which pushed my social interaction thresholds further than I had ever experienced. The work to fix it up seemed to grow every day we stepped into it, stretching my physical limitations to the max. Many days I worked there alone for long stretches of the day. My dad could no longer come to help me. My dad was gone. I am forever grateful to the friends and people of our church who could help and did.

Fueling me forward was the memory of Dad's voice encouraging me to "get that building and move your church into there!" We made it through just in time to celebrate Resurrection Sunday in the new building. How I wished he could stand by my side to celebrate. But I knew, without a doubt, that I had his support.

Alongside of beginning a fundraising campaign to buy a property, I had to plan my dad's memorial service. It was a difficult thing to plan, but it turned out to be a very special time. We didn't have the typical speech. He wouldn't have given one, and often fell asleep during the speeches of others. But we did tell his story since he rarely told it himself. We had short readings accompanied by photos that showed him in the different facets of his life, such as hobbies (cars and trains and such...), being a husband, being a dad, and being a grandpa.

I welcomed folks and helped read some opening reflections. Many parts, though, I knew I wouldn't be able to read. We had a great group of friends and family who stood in and read for my mom and me, and played some songs, old country style. The service was at our church, and a sweet group gathered to remember my dad and comfort the family. One of the things a number of people said to me as they parted was "he was so proud of you." Every time they said it was special, but they didn't have to say it.

During his last weeks with us, several times, he looked up at me and said, "I'm proud of you, son" or "I love you." I kind of knew these things. I'd truly never doubted his love or support, but I had never heard it so many times from his lips. It seemed his top priority before his death was to encourage me deeply. And for that I'll be forever grateful.

12

Come, Lord Jesus

"...let the one who is thirsty come;
let the one who desires
take the water of life without price.
He who testifies to these things says,
'Surely I am coming soon.'
Amen. Come, Lord Jesus!"

Revelation 22:17b, 20 Holy Bible ESV

It surprised me for a second that I was crying...not only crying, but crying with a man I'd just met...crying while mounting a tire.

Dwight and I had started out our first day together in Albany collecting supplies for the old F-250. We'd been over to the auto parts store, where Dwight has an account and better pricing through his farm, to get some gaskets, a carb kit, a gas cap (which we forgot), and some wiper blades. Then we headed over to the town of Stayton to see Dennis, whom Dwight had sworn would have everything we needed.

Indeed he did. There was the set of tires, he'd promised over the phone, on a good-looking set of old Ford rims. We threw out to Dennis that we might need a driver's side exhaust manifold, and he led us back to a truck bed full of manifolds and, sure enough...he found just the one we needed in there. He had previously set aside a pair of working headlights and a battery that was fairly new. We were out the door for only $310.

*Dennis rummages through a truck bed full of
Ford manifolds*

So far we were moving at a pretty steady clip. As we cruised the beautiful Oregon countryside, we tried to map out the game plan on the old truck. We realized that we had forgotten the gas cap...we'd have to go back to town at some point for that...but we figured we might as well make some progress on few of the other projects first.

Wiper blades went on like a snap. By that I mean, I snapped one of the plastic clips right off the "cheap things." Was it cheap? Maybe...but I knew Dwight was bummed we couldn't get the refills for the old metal Trico wipers, so I figured he'd understand if one of these plastic ones broke. And he did. He muttered a bit about the lack of quality parts these days.

We mounted up the battery, swapped the headlights and moved on to rims and tires. Dwight was more than a little unsure of my abilities, and for good reason. I've turned many a wrench in my life, but not nearly as many as he had. He found my lug nuts to be a bit loose for his liking until we got to the last wheel.

As I was lifting the heavy rim and tire up to match the studs to the holes in the rim, he asked... "Your dad die of cancer?"

"Yeah," I said...still fairly in the zone lining up all eight of the studs. I slid the tire on, grabbed the lug nuts out of the hubcap, and started to thread them on with my fingers.

"Mine did too," Dwight said. "What kind?"

"Maybe colon cancer," I told him...stopping a second from my work. "They didn't do an autopsy. It was all over his gut. He wouldn't go to a doctor 'til he couldn't eat. By then it was too late for treatment."

Dwight had a knowing look on his wrinkled face. "That can be a terrible one," he said quietly.

"Yeah...they did surgery to remove the blockage from the intestine and that's when they found it. Doctor came out and said it could be days...or months. We got six more weeks with him. Sometimes that cancer can be a long drawn-out thing."

"Yeah...I was gonna say..." Dwight mumbled.

"They were gonna send him home for home hospice, which worried us all. My mom's limping around. It would have been really hard."

Dwight nods.

"And the worst part was how miserable he was. My dad... the worst thing for my dad...was being laid up in a hospital bed not being able to keep down his food." I've forgotten about the truck. "And you know...when you have that cancer, you basically have to try to eat though it comes back up, and you basically starve."

"It's terrible." Dwight nods.

"So the crazy thing is..." I had to stop. "Excuse me..." My whole body was welling up and I couldn't speak...as if my vocal chords had been clamped shut. I realized it was because I was instinctively trying not to cry in front of this man. "I'm gonna cry just talking about it," I stammered.

"That's OK."

The tears began to fall gently. "I prayed that night..." I continued... "I knew he was so uncomfortable...I prayed that night that God would take him home...you know...and when I got home, not long after, my wife got a phone call. He was gone. Got up to use the restroom, sat back down...and in a second... just the snap of the fingers, he was gone...and when we got to the hospital, my mom told me she'd prayed the same thing. That cancer usually makes you die a slow, miserable death."

Dwight nods. "Sure does."

With kind eyes he hands me the impact wrench, I wipe my eyes on my shirtsleeve and take a deep breath. Time to tighten the bolts. I drive them all in and Dwight checks my work one by one.

"That one's tight...so's that one...and that one's fine. Well... you had 'em all nice and tight that time."

I guess I was getting the hang of all this.

It might seem strange that my mom and I would pray such a thing. Honestly, I've never meant a prayer so much as I meant that one. There's more to the story though.

Those six weeks my dad was in the hospital were so utterly painful that I can hardly stand to write about them. One thing I can say, though, is that I decided to leave nothing unsaid every time I went to see him.

I held his hands, fixed his hair, hugged him, and told him I loved him every time I left the room. I tried to leave no stone unturned. I brought up every memory I had. I asked him every question I could think of. I asked him about how he was feeling about the fact he was going to die soon. I asked him what he wanted me to keep. I asked him what his priorities were for me and for Mom. I told him my deepest hope for him was that, in his death, he'd be able to know God like a father and feel a father's love the way he'd never gotten to experience it in his life. I could hardly speak those words. His eyes were gentle, full of tears.

In one of those conversations I asked him if he was afraid to die. He said... "Oh I don't know...I try not to think about it too much."

I asked him if there was anything he was praying about through all of this.

He paused... "Oh...what do you say? Just...come, Lord Jesus."

I knew exactly what he meant. He'd read his Bible so many times. He was interested in what the last book meant. In fact, we'd had a disagreement about portions of it on one of our walks through the neighborhood not too long back. I asked him to read a book I had that interpreted Revelation differently than the ways he'd heard in the churches we went to when I was a kid and on TV. He said he would read the book, and he did. He gave it back completed within a week or two. He said it was interesting.

The great hope at the end of the Bible is that God has had a plan all along, which includes every created thing being restored and renewed for the enjoyment of those who have received his grace. This hope includes the undoing of death for those who trusted God's good plan and his savior-son Jesus.

All of this was revealed in an incredible vision to John, one of Jesus' closest disciples. In conclusion to his book, John simply utters a prayer... "Amen (So shall it be), Come, Lord Jesus." That's all my dad knew to say. And if after stunning visions of heavenly things, that's all the Apostle John had to say...then I suppose my dad's prayer was about right.

So, when my mom and I prayed that Jesus would come and take my dad's person from his body to await that final day...it was in keeping with the very hope my dad clung to amidst all of his doubts. I've never prayed such a heartfelt prayer. And I thank God every time I remember that Jesus came and took my daddy from his misery early.

The day I drove out to the Oregon coast couldn't have been more beautiful. The sky was grey and misty, but it wasn't quite raining. The air was crisp and cool, but it wasn't cold. It was perfect light-jacket weather...the kind when you can wear your jacket to keep warm, but you never get too hot. I was able to drive through the forests with the windows down and able to walk in the foamy ocean water as it washed across the rough sand beaches. I'd once asked my dad where his favorite place to walk was, and this was it. I couldn't blame him.

My experience of walking the beach had come mostly from California, Florida and the Bahamas. Those beaches are undeniably beautiful, but the crowd gets to me. The last thing I feel like doing is taking off ninety percent of my clothes and sitting around with a bunch of people who've taken off most of their clothing too. The second to last thing I want to do is lay around on a towel. Every time I've gone to the beach somewhere I've been inclined to start walking instead of taking part in all that.

Walking the Oregon coast, at least these parts, was completely different. The photos I'd seen of my dad doing it usually captured him nearly alone, in his typical flannel and pleated pants, just gazing out into a vast grey ocean with tree lined beaches behind him. That was my experience, too. The people who were out there were mostly searching the sand for agates or gathering with friends to make driftwood fires. Their full outfits were still intact except their shoes in some cases.

Some houseless folks had taken up residence on the beaches in driftwood structures with fires going at their front entrances. People here were just living life in the presence of this mighty body of water. It was peaceful and you felt at home. I could completely understand the urge to set up a driftwood lean-to...I wanted to wake up to this every morning myself.

The hard part, of course, was the realization that I never got to take my dad's favorite walk with him. He would have loved to share the experience with me, but we didn't know how short on time we were. Over and over my eyes would swell with tears as I'd imagine he was there with me...wishing I could reach my hand out and touch his shoulder...wishing I could sit on a rock and watch him sift the surf-washed stones for agates. I wished we could talk about the old truck I'd just found and make plans to pull the Model A around with it. I wished we could grab a cup of coffee to sip as we quietly made our way back to the truck from a nice day on the ocean together.

Years back I worked at a small neighborhood church and a young kid from the neighborhood would always come around after school. He didn't know his dad and had a long list of hurtful experiences with the other men that had been in his life. He and I became kind of a team. He would tag around with me after school and help me work on my truck on the weekends. I made sure he got his homework done, and once a week we would go out for a walk to get a coffee and read the Bible. After coffee we would play a game of basketball down at the courts under the shade of the University of Arizona football stadium.

One day he asked if he could show me his favorite verse as he flipped through the little Bible I'd bought for him. He, to my surprise, flipped back to the book of Revelation, Chapter 21.

"Then I saw a new heaven and a new earth. The first heaven and the first earth had disappeared, and there was no sea anymore. And I saw the holy city, the new Jerusalem, coming down out of heaven from God. It was prepared like a bride dressed for her husband. And I heard a loud voice from the throne, saying, "Now God's presence is with people and he will live with them, and they will be his people. God himself will be with them and will be their God. He will wipe away every tear from their eyes, and there will be no more death, sadness, crying or pain, because all of the old ways are gone." -- Revelation 21:1-4 NCV

This young guy's life had been so hard. He, his sister and his mom had shed so many tears. It must have been so good to hear that one day the sadness and pain would end. It must have been comforting to hear that it isn't all for nothing. In his own way this kid was saying, "Come, Lord Jesus!"

In hanging out with me so much, the kid also got to meet my dad. You could tell they liked each other. One time I shared my dad's story with him. I showed him how my dad's faith, along with some key choices, shaped him into being a better man than he had been taught to be. From that day on I could tell that he looked up to my dad more. He didn't need a hero who hadn't suffered and had it all together. He needed to see that someone small and imperfect could have hope and move forward despite all that evidence to the contrary.

My hazy day on the Oregon Coast

As I walked down the beach on that cool spring day in Oregon, I, too, thought about Revelation 21. I would never pretend to know exactly how to sort out that book's imagery and meaning perfectly, but I thought about how good it all sounded.

There are options I know. Many of my friends are convinced that when you die, you're dead, and that's that. They don't believe there's anything more, or that this life leads to another, or that there's some kind of transcendent meaning to the love and beauty we experience in our lives. I can see how they come to those conclusions, but it's hard for me to understand how life's worth living when that's all you've got.

My mind went to a place of imagining again. I imagined a day when the "old ways are gone." I imagined knowing my dad, but a version of him that had experienced the presence of God the Father in his life. I imagined him without all the self-doubt, with a confidence that came from daily fatherly affirmations that sunk all the way down to the core of his heart. I imagined walking with him in the beauty of creation... perhaps on the Oregon Coast...made perfect.

None of the people who lived on the beach were there because they had no choice. They were there just because it was beautiful.

I imagined that Dad and I were getting back to the business we'd begun in our lifetimes. We talked about our wives and my daughter and the glorious women they'd become. We talked about our projects and getting back to work on them. We'd have to go find a trailer to hook up to that old F-250 so we could travel together...the Model A was running like a dream.

I realize that I have no clue what things one might do in the new heavens and new earth. I know I can't prove they're going to come to pass. But I do know how right it would be because I felt it in that moment as I walked. I had to stop and talk to my Father in heaven. My simple prayer was, "God, that would be so good." And for the first time in a long time, I began to well up with tears of joy. I've never been a very emotional guy, but the thought of that kind of hope made my heart soar. It turned my sadness into a longing; "Come, Lord Jesus!"

The days after my dad died, our family experienced an unexplainable peace. We had asked Jesus to come and take Dad for now, and he had. Watching him dying of cancer had been so hard, and so wrong. Of course, our hearts were full of pain. We would miss him terribly. No family gathering would ever be the same...no breakfast out...no walk around the neighborhood.

We were feeling the pain so many of our friends had felt in some measure. My wife's and my closest friends had lost their triplets at birth not long back. The family of a pastor friend had recently awakened to find their child dead in the night. The young husband and father of a family in our church was diagnosed with cancer and died not long before that. Death feels anything but natural.

One night as my wife, Michaela, and I tucked my daughter into bed; we sang the songs we sing together every bedtime. We start with You Are My Sunshine and end with He's Got the Whole World in His Hands. Our version of He's Got the Whole World in His Hands includes the names of a bunch of our closest friends and their families. Five of the names we were now singing were those who had died.

My daughter was thinking a lot about death, wondering if I was going to die of cancer, too. I told her we didn't know, but there are things God does tell us we can know...and that's that someday all the death and sadness will stop, and things will be the way they ought to be.

I remembered another portion of the Bible that cast the beautiful vision hundreds of years before John, the disciple of Jesus, had his...

"For behold, I create a new heavens and a new earth, and the former things shall not be remembered or come into mind. But be glad and rejoice forever in that which I create; for behold, I create Jerusalem to be joy, and her people to be a gladness. I will rejoice in Jerusalem and be glad in my people; no more shall be heard in it the sound of weeping and the cry of distress. No more shall there be in it an infant who lives but a few days, or an old man who does not fill out his days..." Isaiah 65:17-20a ESV

As I read that, Abby stopped me...

"That's like papa. He wanted to live longer."

"Yeah, sweetie, it is."

"And like the triplets...and Jay..."

"Yeah, it is sweetie. But that won't happen anymore someday... and they'll all be there with us."

She let out a peaceful sigh and rolled over...she could sleep. Things were going to turn out all right in the end. She could live with that.

13
There Are Others

The day after Thanksgiving, 11 days after my dad died, I drove down to Bisbee. I walked up Main Street once but knew immediately I'd come to the wrong part of town. The streets were bursting with tourists and shoppers there for the holiday weekend. The locals were in hiding. Hiding already sounded best to me, too. I was not in the market for crowds. I'd hoped to experience the Bisbee my dad and I would have shared on a visit.

The family had long ago built a patchwork house out on the old homestead outside of Bisbee. Dad said the foundation was railroad ties and that they built the house out of whatever they could get. That's the Bisbee I grew up visiting most. The shoppers' paradise of Old Bisbee merely served as a place to pause on our way in or out.

The old house had a small vegetable garden and a massive windmill, but the most prominent yard articles were the cars. Dozens of cars. My grandpa let someone store a bunch of antique cars out in the surrounding brush. I suppose a few cars once belonged to the family but just got kept around like the

Model A had been. My Uncle Jake went with the trend and started storing vehicles he found to sell for parts or scrap metal.

As I walked Old Bisbee's main street, I began to desire to get out...out to the outskirts...to where my dad had walked the dirt roads and hunted for arrowheads. I made some phone calls, but nobody, not even my aunt who grew up there too and lived only minutes away, knew the house's exact address. A couple more attempts fell flat, so I just began to drive, looking for landmarks I'd last seen in my 20's when my dad and I last visited my uncle.

First came a sign for Double Adobe, the "inhabited place" name for the area where the family had lived, near an archaeological site that had been discovered in 1926 by a schoolboy. I had to be on the right track now. Then there was a dilapidated sign pointing to a now-closed bar and steakhouse I vaguely remembered as well. Next came the metal garage with the large words "KEEP OUT" sprayed prominently on the front bay that set not far off the road surrounded by rubbish... also very familiar. Last, a strange old scrap metal cowboy mailbox. That rang a bell. I knew my turn was coming up.

The terrain began to look increasingly familiar. Memories flooded back from when our family lived out there for a while in our motor home, and my dad would walk me through the desert to look for arrowheads like he did as a kid. I never found one, but I did find a stone pestle, so worn down by an ancient hand that my fingers slid right into place.

I remembered how my dad and I would smash out the windshields of the old cars destined for meltdown at the scrap yard. "Where else could we do this and nobody care?" reasoned Dad. We'd lob the biggest rocks we could through the windows. The crash and shatter echoed across the arid landscape, and nobody cared. The crevices cut in the earth by the rain water reminded me of how I imagined my dad and I were traversing canyons together as we'd find our way back to the old house.

The next flood of thoughts was not so much memories

as imaginations. I began to imagine my dad as a teenager wandering these remote streets alone on a lazy afternoon. I imagined the days his dad's contemptuous eyes drove the deep insecurities he'd struggled with deeper into his heart. I imagined a skinny kid like me lost in his thoughts, wishing he wasn't so weak and slow. A kid wishing he could relate to his dad, or to anyone. I imagined him, eyes to the dirt, kicking rocks as he tried to figure out how to feel about it all.

About then I drove up to a row of mailboxes I recognized, and I knew I had arrived. Here was the rugged old driveway we'd driven our motor home down so slowly. The one that the dogs would run down to meet us. Ahead I saw the windmill towering over the tired old structure, surrounded by acres of vehicle carcasses, tires, and dilapidated mobile homes.

I slowed my truck, creeping up the driveway hesitantly. Finally I worked up the courage to get out and initiate contact with my Uncle Jake, my dad's younger brother who had stayed out on the property after the rest of the family had either moved on or died. A light was on...only the screen door was closed, but nobody answered. I figured I'd better head back.

The old, family homestead

At day's end, back in Old Bisbee, I sat down to reflect. Tears welled up in my eyes at the thought of my dad as a child. I can't begin to understand the extent of the damage. Then it hit me. I have so often been the one filled with contempt toward people like my dad. Especially as a younger man, feeling weak and small myself, I'd treated some people really poorly. Maybe that's why my grandpa gave my dad such a hard time. Maybe he was kind of like me. I don't know, but the thought that I've damaged children like my dad in my past brought on a wave of regret. I can't go back. I can't undo the damage.

My dad grew into a kind and respectable man. One I'm deeply proud to claim as my own. From time to time he'd mention someone who treated him kindly on his journey through life. There was the neighbor who taught him guitar as a kid, a close friend he enjoyed working with on his hobbies, a co-worker who he'd enjoy "giving a hard time". The list wasn't too long, but I'm deeply grateful for every one of them. They shaped my life by loving my dad well during his.

There are others like my dad. Too many to count, I suppose. A downcast young man gave me a sideways glare at the coffee shop in Old Bisbee. I'd seen him out on the sidewalk playing an acoustic bass guitar, trying to bum a cigarette off a passerby. I wonder who taught him to play his instrument. I wonder what his father is like. I wonder if he even knows him. There are others, too. Many I know.

In my church we have a number of friends that aren't arriving with any money to give or the personality that gets one involved. I'm so glad they are with us. Many a big-talker has come and gone...many a potential donor. But I would be proud to have a church full of Leroys. By God's grace we will.

There are others. You know them, too. The quiet kid. The disabled woman. Those unsure of themselves most of the time. The ones that come across as faithless. Love them, please! Love them because some of us are too stupid and self-centered to consider them more valuable than ourselves right now. Love them because it is so easy to pass them by, or worse, to demean them for the millionth time. Love them because they may prove to love you deeply, and you'll find that you received a gift from God the day you invited them into your life. Love them because in loving them you love God, no matter the perceivable result.

At Jesse's church in Naco, a small group showed up early for a Bible study before church. An older Anglo woman was there early, as well as a well-dressed and well-spoken Hispanic man who spoke little English. Eventually another older lady snuck in late. The Bible study focused on a Proverb, and the discussion turned to helping others and exercising wisdom in doing so. A brief mention was made concerning drug addictions. The lady who had come in late spoke up saying, "We always have to remember that we're no better than those people addicted to drugs."

After the study I made introductions and asked how each of them ended up in the area. The lady who spoke up told me she had lived in Old Bisbee a long time. Like my mom, she used to own a small independent bookstore. Unlike my mom, she married a man who didn't treat her well.

She said she'd always seen the down-and-out folks around town and figured that they had some kind of issues unlike her. She subtly looked down on them. Then her marriage had gone south, and she was unhappy. She slipped into drug use...she was an old child of the 60's. She had no religious convictions anchoring her. She had just run on being a good person, but that ship had sailed. Her life unravelled and she lost everything. I asked her what had brought her to the church.

"Well," she said, "God had to bring me low."

She had lost everything, and a pastor lady in Old Bisbee showed her compassion and took her in to her house. She was taken aback by the generosity and began to consider that maybe she needed God. Eventually she'd moved down by the border where it cost less.

She missed Old Bisbee but had found a great little church and a pastor that liked books like she did. She was reading Tim Keller at Jesse's suggestion, and had just discovered Eugene Peterson and loved his spiritual insight.

Someone loved her when she was at her worst, and God had brought her through the valley of the shadow of death into fields of green she'd never seen before. She was grateful for the whole journey.

At Jesse's house church in Sonora, Mexico, a man in a wheel chair asked me, in perfect English, what I was doing on my sabbatical. I told him about taking time to work on a writing project about my dad. I'd hardly begun to explain it to him when tears filled his eyes.

"I wish my son would write something like that about me."

"I take it you two aren't close?" I offered.

"No, he doesn't want anything to do with me."

He went on to explain that he'd been a drinker. He'd work long hard days and then go out to drink before coming home.

It kind of sounded like my grandpa.

He'd since eased the drinking way back, he said, and a near-fatal injury had confined him to a wheel chair. He was sorry for the way he'd neglected his family. He'd asked for forgiveness but, so far, things were still no good with his son.

We prayed together that he and his son might have a second chance...hopeful because they still had time. For now, though, he did have a church family. The kids from the orphanage seemed to love being around him. He shared an idea he had... to have them all over to his place for a barbecue. He beamed with pride that he was able to help out at the church and make a difference. The church had been a huge help in his life.

My dad never heard an "I'm sorry" from his father. They never really patched things up. I don't believe my dad felt his father loved him and, for that, I'm very sad.

I have heard that my grandfather eased back on his drinking, too, and perhaps even quit altogether. I've heard that one of his granddaughters was going down a similar path, and that he took her out for a walk in his vegetable garden and told her that the drinking could lead her to some things she'd really regret. She listened to his advice. I'm sure pride kept him from making all of his amends, but it does help to know that he wasn't a lost cause. Even he was able to change. I suppose anybody can. Imagine if someone had been more involved in his life, encouraging him...what a difference it could have made.

You don't have to be loud or be a big shot to make an impact on the world. I hope you see that in the pages of this book.

Sometimes we get so caught up listening to the loudest voices that we forget the impact of our own life upon the lives of others...for better or worse.

Sometimes we get so caught up in ourselves that we miss the chance to get to know someone very special or invest the time into the relationships in front of us.

Sometimes we're listening to so many experts that we forget to listen to someone who's just kind of lived life. Maybe they know a lot more than we think. And maybe the people being paid to talk a lot don't know so much after all. Let me tell you...I get paid to talk sometimes. I sure don't know it all by any stretch of the imagination. And...I wish you all could have gotten to know my quiet Dad.

My dad told me he loved me so many times as he lay on the bed in the hospital waiting to die. He said it out loud. He said it in the way he looked at me. He said it when he squeezed my hand. But, he didn't have to say it. My whole life I knew I was safe in his love. Boy, did he struggle! Often he didn't love himself and failed to love others like he should have. Boy, did he blow it sometimes! But I always knew that he loved me.

I work with a lot of men and I realize now what a gift I was given by God. That gift was given through a little man. By a man almost destroyed. By a man almost completely passed over by the hordes of humanity looking for their heart's desires. My dad was a gift of God's grace. I truly didn't deserve him.

There are others. Love them. Seek them out. Take the time to get to know them, as difficult as that may be. Fill your churches with them. Bring them into your homes and spend time in theirs, even if you're nervous about crossing the threshold of a mobile home. In it may be a gift. A friend who sticks closer than a brother. Somebody's father.

"Long live the little man.
God bless the little man."
Alan Jackson - Little Man

Appendix I
People

One of my favorite pictures of Dad
later in life

*Betty Bowles at the Odyssey Book Shop
in Lebanon, Oregon.*

Leroy and Betty Littleton, the cute young couple.

Dwight gazing out across the Santiam River from the back of his property.

Appendix II
Places

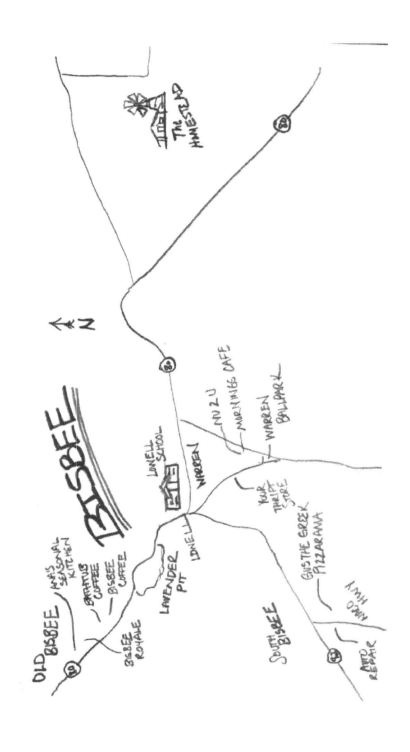

Quick Facts:

Bisbee is a little mining town tucked into Tombstone Canyon amidst Southern Arizona's Mule Mountains. It was bustling and full of life while the copper mines were active, but today it's slowed down. It's still an incredible town with beautiful old storefronts lining the winding streets. Miner's shacks hang off the sides of the steep hills like Christmas tree ornaments connected by crooked runs of concrete stairs. A massive open pit mine careens downward from the edge of the old city; the Lavender Pit. Bisbee was connected to a number of neighboring towns; Lowell, Jiggerville, and Warren to name a few. It is the birthplace of Leroy Littleton Jr.

Andy's Fav Dining Spots:

1. Ana's Seasonal Kitchen - breakfast sandwich + coffee (sadly now closed)
2. Gus the Greek - Pizzarama - pizza and an RC Cola
3. Morning's Cafe in Warren - omelet and coffee

Andy's Fav Activities:

1. Walking Tombstone Canyon (Old Bisbee)
2. Thrifting in Warren - Nu 2 U + Your Thrift Store
3. Copper City Classic Vintage Baseball Tournament - Warren Ballpark
4. 4th of July - Vista Park

LEBANON

↗ "THE SWAMP"

↑ "WINDY HILL"

TO ALBANY ↑

30

The Lobby

KORNER KITCHEN

ODYSSEY BOOK SHOP (formerly)

N ←

34

5

S. LEBANON

DAD'S WALK

Sodaville

Quick Facts:

Lebanon is a small town, a bit off the beaten path, about twenty-five minutes west of Albany. It boomed when lumber was a bigger and less regulated industry in Oregon. It got hit hard when the spotted owl was first protected and logging was reigned in. I hear from folks at our old church that it's now growing again. The lush green hills topped with regal pine trees in perfect formation, sprinkled with a white and yellow confetti of wild flowers, have a way of capturing you. You do though...have to watch out for cougars.

Andy's Fav Dining Spots:

1. Korner Kitchen - omelet + coffee + morning paper (sadly now closed)
2. The Lobby - coffee + strawberry shortcake (I had to special order)

Andy's Fav Activities:

1. Walking from Sodaville to South Lebanon
2. Thrifting
3. Eating fresh strawberries (Lebanon Strawberry Festival in June or at the farmer's markets downtown)

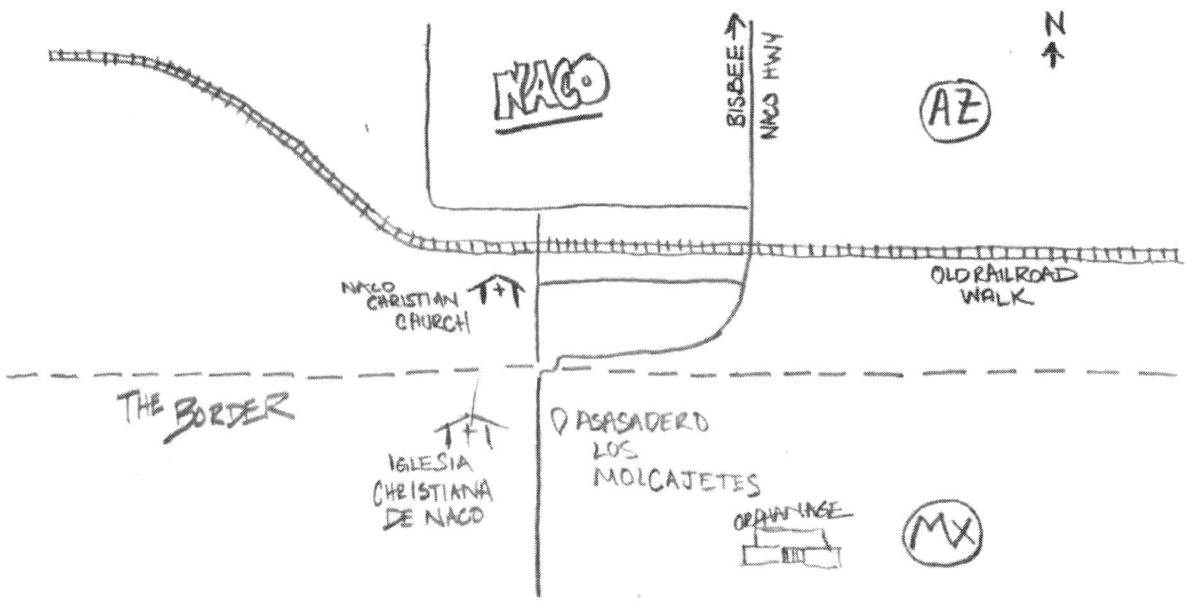
N
NACO
BISBEE
NACO HWY
AZ
OLD RAILROAD WALK
NACO CHRISTIAN CHURCH
THE BORDER
IGLESIA CHRISTIANA DE NACO
ASASADERO LOS MOLCAJETES
ORPHANAGE
MX

Quick Facts:

Naco is the smallest of the border towns with a Port of Entry. It's an "unincorporated place" on the U.S. side with very few remaining businesses. It used to boast a popular automotive reconditioning shop that fueled the tiny economy. The Gay 90's bar is the only old business that's still hanging in there. It was named back in 1931 when the word gay meant lighthearted. You can see the old port of entry and Tom Waits doing sit-ups outside the window of a moving car in the movie Cold Feet (1989). The surprised looking family in the car next to Tom's still live in Naco. It's a good size town on the Sonora, Mexico side with a baseball stadium, industry and busy restaurants and shops.

Andy's Fav Dining Spots:

1. Asadero Los Molcajetes - Naco, Sonora - tacos and Coke

Andy's Fav Activities:

1. Naco Christian Church - Sunday Service
2. Walking down the old railroad tracks.

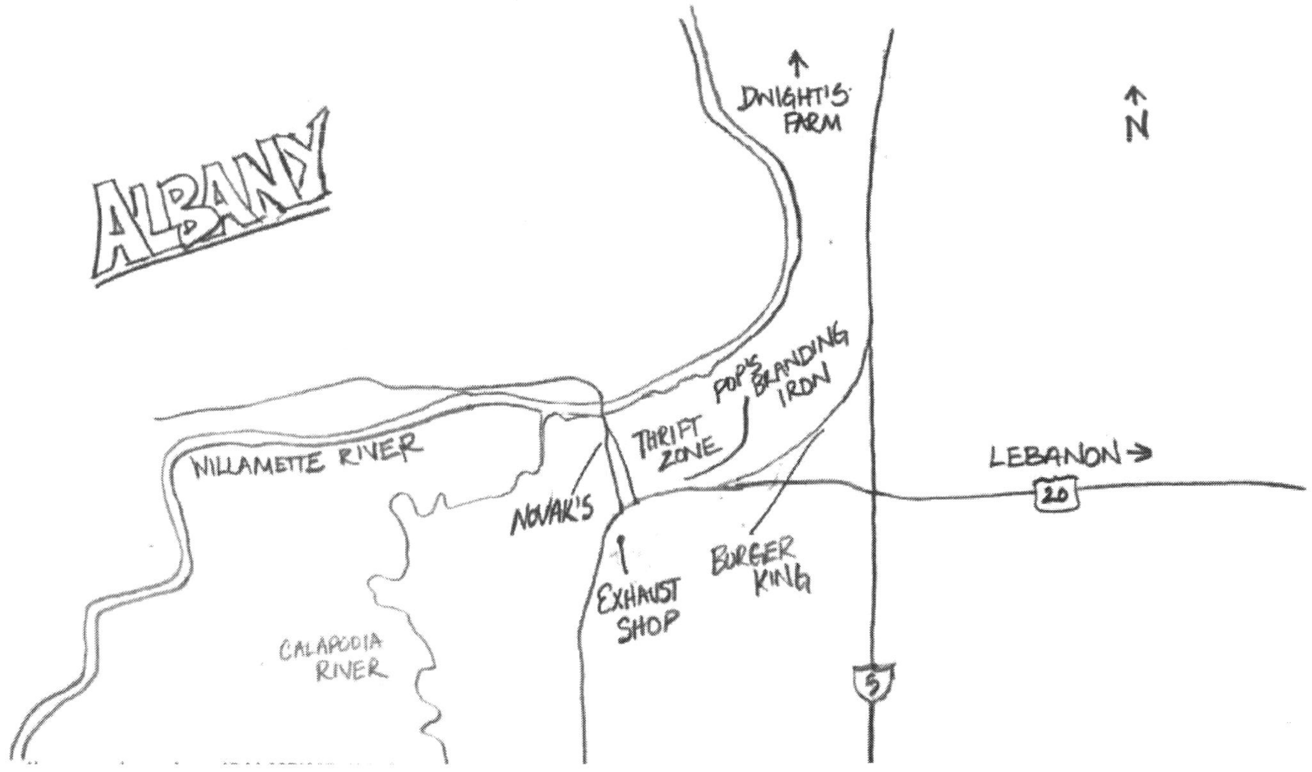
ALBANY
DWIGHT'S FARM
N
POP'S BRANDING IRON
THRIFT ZONE
LEBANON
20
WILLAMETTE RIVER
NOVAK'S
BURGER KING
EXHAUST SHOP
CALAPOOIA RIVER
5

Quick Facts:

Settlers founded Albany back in 1848 because it was a great area for farming and manufacturing. It's located where the Calapooia and Willamette rivers converge. It's still surrounded by farms like Dwight's and a number of factories. The city has become known for hosting cultural events. Back when I was a kid, our family would attend the Timber Carnival in Albany. That event has since been discontinued.

Andy's Fav Dining Spots:

1. Novak's Hungarian Restaurant - Reggeli (breakfast menu)
2. Burgerville - burger + fries (Oregon chain that's great! - It's a waste of money in Dwight's opinion, though I swear it costs the same as Burger King.)
3. Pop's Branding Iron - Hot Roast Beef
4. Burger King - Whopper + soda - Dwight's go-to meal

Andy's Fav Activities:

1. Bryant Park - staring at the Calapooia and Willamette rivers.
2. Thrifting - Teen Challenge + St. Vinny's + Goodwill + Albany Helping Hands

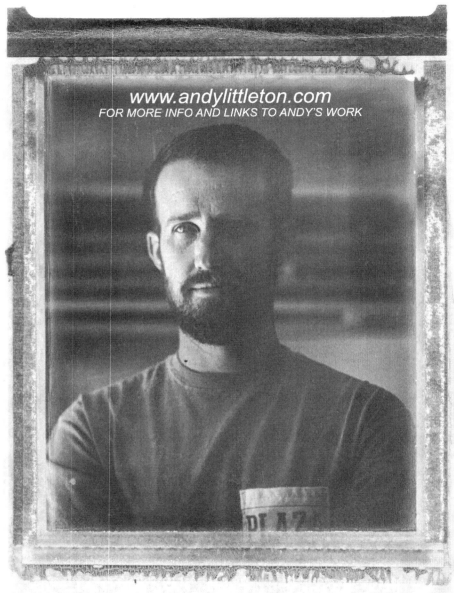

www.andylittleton.com
FOR MORE INFO AND LINKS TO ANDY'S WORK

Vintage Poloroid Image Courtesy of Stephen Thomas - stephenthomas.co

Made in the USA
Las Vegas, NV
06 December 2022

61309142R00104